Bodice Engineering

Bodice Engineering

Mastering the Inner Corselette

Louise Johnson

BLOOMSBURY VISUAL ARTS
LONDON • NEW YORK • OXFORD • NEW DELHI • SYDNEY

BLOOMSBURY VISUAL ARTS
Bloomsbury Publishing Plc, 50 Bedford Square, London, WC1B 3DP, UK
Bloomsbury Publishing Inc, 1359 Broadway, New York, NY 10018, USA
Bloomsbury Publishing Ireland, 29 Earlsfort Terrace, Dublin 2, D02 AY28, Ireland

BLOOMSBURY, BLOOMSBURY VISUAL ARTS and the Diana logo are trademarks of Bloomsbury Publishing Plc

First published in Great Britain 2026

A catalogue record for this book is available from the British Library.

Library of Congress Cataloging-in-Publication Data

Names: Johnson, Louise (Dressmaker) author
Title: Bodice engineering : mastering the inner corselette / Louise Johnson.
Description: London ; New York : Bloomsbury Visual Arts, 2026. | Includes bibliographical references and index. | Summary: "In this practical guide, experienced couture dressmaker Louise Johnson introduces the fundamental techniques required to design and sew an inner corselette. In part one, step-by-step instructions demonstrate the process of building an inner corselette, while part two unpicks the construction of six existing garments"– Provided by publisher.
Identifiers: LCCN 2025026546 | ISBN 9781350537170 hardback | ISBN 9781350537163 paperback | ISBN 9781350537187 ePDF | ISBN 9781350537194 eBook
Subjects: LCSH: Corsets–Patterns | Dresses | Fashion design
Classification: LCC TT677 .J64 2026
LC record available at https://lccn.loc.gov/2025026546

ISBN: PB: 978-1-3505-3716-3
ePDF: 978-1-3505-3718-7
eBook: 978-1-3505-3719-4

Typeset by Integra Software Services Pvt. Ltd.
Printed and bound in India

For product safety related questions contact productsafety@bloomsbury.com.

To find out more about our authors and books visit www.bloomsbury.com and sign up for our newsletters.

Contents

Preface

I've been fascinated with fashion, particularly the styles from the 1950s, for as long as I can remember. The alluring gowns with figure-hugging bodices, nipped-in waists and voluminous skirts supported by layers and layers of tulle transport me to a time when life seemed to exist in a perpetual state of glamour. Whenever I see such elegant gowns, I am in awe of their beauty and, at the same time, immediately curious about what lies beneath the beautiful fabrics. What invisible structures support the designs to make them appear so effortlessly elegant?

For many years I searched in vain for a book that would show me the secrets of these gowns, in particular the inner corselette, which I have long admired. But where do you find a pattern? How should a corselette fit properly and what is the best fabric to use? What boning choices are there and where does the boning go? How does the corselette join to the garment? The questions seemed endless.

I realized that I would need to do my own research to find the answers. This led me on an amazing journey I couldn't have imagined at the start. I began by exploring the history and construction of the corset, from which the inner corselette evolved many decades ago. Then I turned my attention to vintage dressmaking patterns, dating back to a time when the inner corselette first emerged. These gave insight into techniques not seen in modern patterns. Reading books on historical patterns and sewing techniques, haute couture designs and the history and construction of lingerie also added to my knowledge. And, of course, I've experimented with sewing inner corselettes using different fabrics, boning, fastenings and construction methods. Through a combination of following pattern instructions and trial and error, I gained experience with the techniques. I also developed an understanding of the reasons behind the effectiveness of different construction methods.

As you can imagine, the scope of this field is broad, and it is impossible for this book to include every technique for all eventualities. What I have included are the most commonly used techniques and methods that will allow most projects to be undertaken with great success. Some techniques have not been described in literature previously, except as steps on a pattern instruction sheet, and so do not have names. I have therefore taken the liberty of categorizing and naming these in a way that seems logical to me and makes referencing them easier.

You will notice that a lot of hand-sewing and couture techniques are used in these projects. I personally find this type of sewing enjoyable, but, most importantly, I love the high-quality results. If you are not familiar with these techniques, I encourage you to spend some time learning them. In many cases, however, the techniques can be applied to the projects in a way you see fit.

The book is divided into two parts. Part One introduces the inner corselette and shows a standard design and construction method, as well as a range of variations. There is detailed information on selecting, adjusting and fitting a corselette pattern, choosing and installing the boning and fastening, and incorporating the corselette into your garment.

Part Two provides a step-by-step guide through the construction of six inner corselettes. With each project, you will follow the process from selecting and fitting the pattern to constructing the corselette and the garment and finally joining them together. Each inner corselette uses a different combination of fabric, boning, fastenings, edge treatments and joining methods, with detailed information about the construction process.

I have written this book to share my findings in my own search for knowledge, and to give others the confidence to start their own journey into creating an inner corselette. Your first corselette is unlikely to be perfect; neither was mine. Start slowly with a simple project and give yourself time and patience to build your skills. Endless combinations of features are possible on an inner corselette and are limited only by your imagination. I hope that this book sparks in you a new passion that you find as exciting and rewarding as I have.

Foreword

When I was a little girl, there was a big cardboard box in the attic. It contained the dresses that my mother had worn to dances at the country club, and it seemed as if there were acres of tulle and taffeta in the prettiest of colours: soft pink, peach, mint green, royal blue, all there for my sister and me to play with. This was the 1950s, and, of course, what I was unaware of at the time was the engineering that went into those dresses, with their tight strapless bodices and their full, fluffy skirts.

And who hasn't looked at a fabulous couture confection (yes, that's what they call them in Paris – *confections* … how perfect …) and wondered just what goes on inside … what sleight-of-hand, what alchemy, what engineering is beneath it all, keeping everything so elegantly and securely shaped?

Whether you'd simply like to know just how those dresses stay in place (and let's face it, who wouldn't?), or whether you want to create one of your own, help is at hand. Fortunately, Louise Johnson – a dressmaker with the brain of an engineer – has asked herself the same questions, and she's done all the hard work for you. She's put together a logical, well-thought-out, organized guide that covers all you need to know, from beginning to end, from choosing a pattern to applying the finishing touches.

With the help of *Bodice Engineering: Mastering the Inner Corselette*, you can dream and then design, knowing that, with Louise's help, you've got just what you need to make the magic work.

Susan Khalje, contributing editor of *Threads* magazine and author of *Bridal Couture: Fine Sewing Techniques for Wedding Gowns and Evening Wear.*

Acknowledgements

Taking a book from conception to publication requires the contribution of many people, and wouldn't be possible without their expert assistance and guidance. While creating *Bodice Engineering: Mastering the Inner Corselette*, I worked with an amazing team and I am deeply grateful to all of them.

First, I would like to extend a heartfelt thank-you to Susan Khalje, who encouraged me to write this book. I am truly grateful for her expertise, advice and ongoing encouragement, which has been invaluable to me throughout this journey.

Special thanks must go to Becky Chilcott and her team at Chil3 for their wealth of experience, guidance and attention to detail, which I could not have managed without. Many thanks to my photographer, Sabine Albers, who styled and captured my work so beautifully. My gratitude also extends to Jade Foo for her skill in transforming my sketches and images into works of art.

I am also indebted to Soraya K. McMahon and Rachel Hanson who skilfully polished the manuscript and Lynda Maynard who provided valuable feedback on the technical elements. I thank you all for your expertise, which was essential for shaping my book into clear and eloquent work.

Final thanks go to my family for their constant encouragement, support and belief in the book. Their willingness to help, whether it was giving creative suggestions, offering an extra pair of hands or patiently providing technical advice, will be forever appreciated.

Part One

Building an Inner Corselette

While it may seem complicated, building an inner corselette is a process much like any other in sewing. Some techniques may be new, while others will be familiar, but they're not difficult and the final result is rewarding. This part will guide you through the steps, giving you the essential tools you need to develop your skills. You'll begin by learning to design and fit a corselette using commercial patterns. Then we'll explore the elements needed to complete your project. Next, follow along as we build the corselette step-by-step: constructing the shell; adding the boning and fastenings; and, finally, joining the corselette and the gown.

1

Creating Shape: A Brief History

Throughout history, women have been using undergarments to support and reshape their physiques. Waistlines have been reduced, breasts uplifted or flattened, and hips exaggerated, all in the name of fashion. The ever-evolving corset has played a central role in women's undergarments, supporting and shaping the female body for 500 years. Follow this historical journey to see how undergarment designs and construction methods have changed over time: adapting to new fashion silhouettes and technological advances, in addition to reflecting women's changing roles in society. Importantly, in this chapter you will learn about the emergence of the inner corselette and why it came to be integrated into gowns. Discover its traditional design features and become familiar with its advantages, as well as when to consider building an inner corselette into a design of your own.

The corset, in its earliest form, emerged in the sixteenth century. Called a 'pair of bodys', its simple design consisted of two fabric layers stitched together, often stiffened with paste, and fitted at the waist. A busk in the front kept everything rigid as it smoothed the torso, making the bust appear fuller and the waist smaller. Later, whalebone – also called stays – was incorporated to further reinforce and stiffen the garment and the garment became known as a 'pair of stays'.

Over the ensuing centuries, changes in fashion, technology and skills resulted in changes to the way stays were constructed. Corsetiers experimented with seaming variations and positioning of the whalebones to achieve the ideal silhouettes of the time. Designs were adapted to accommodate average and fuller figures and, towards the end of the 1700s, shaping was built into stays with a hot iron.

By the 1800s, the term 'stays' was replaced with 'corset' as a new silhouette emerged. Aiming to create curves – often dramatic ones – corsets used bust and hip gussets to accommodate the body curves. Later, multiple shaped panels were added. More advances in technology led to changes in the ways corsets were manufactured: coutil replaced stiffened fabric, whalebone was replaced with spiral steel bones, metal eyelets and steel busks were developed and corsets were shaped with steam. However, corsets became heavier and more restrictive, creating exaggerated curves and concern developed for women's health.

Then came the twentieth century. The heavily corseted figure became undesirable as women sought more freedom of movement. Clothing shapes relaxed and undergarments followed suit. Emphasis shifted from creating curves to eliminating them. Corsets became longer to slim the hips and thighs and fell below the bust towards waist level, becoming a predecessor of the girdle. For modesty, simple bandeau brassieres were worn to cover the now exposed breasts. Their simple design merely contained and flattened the breasts, creating the fashionable tubular silhouette.

Soon, the brassiere and the girdle were combined into a single garment – the corselette. Marketed for the mature figure to prevent the undesirable roll of fat that often formed between two separate garments, the corselette was a lighter, more flexible version of the corset. Early styles were in non-stretch fabrics with elastic gussets for movement, had little or no boning, and ended at the low hip with attached garters (Figure 1.1).

By the 1930s, a more natural silhouette was regaining popularity. Bras and corselettes began to include pockets for the breasts and corselette designs now provided gentle figure shaping that highlighted the waist (Figure 1.2). Corselettes were promoted as providing control and shaping, as well as offering a smooth line under the fashionable, figure-hugging evening gowns. The term 'corset', with its negative connotations, was abandoned, and the foundation garment was born.

Figure 1.1 'College Girl' corset designed to flatten the figure to achieve the 1920s straight silhouette. The fabric is non-stretch with elastic hip gores and a side front closure with nineteen hooks and eyes. Two vertical bones in the back and three horizontal bones across the abdomen provide light support (author's collection).

Figure 1.2 Produced by the Standard Co., this corset creates the natural silhouette that was desirable in the 1930s. It provides more figure shaping with separate bra cups, three front bones and four pairs of bones in the back. Made from sturdy cotton and five elastic gussets, there is a side closure with seventeen hooks and eyes (author's collection).

Corselettes and Dior's 'New Look'

This more natural form dominated fashion until 1947, when Christian Dior revived the classic hourglass silhouette. His Corolle collection, or 'New Look' as it was called, brought back close-fitting bodices, nipped-in waists and full skirts, giving the illusion of curves. To enhance the silhouette, Dior revived corsetry and the hourglass shape was cleverly achieved with waist-cinching corselettes, hip padding and skirt stiffening built into the dresses.

The silhouette quickly gained popularity and ready-to-wear copies appeared around the world. These copies needed to be worn over separate foundation garments to create the fashionable shape. New styles of foundation garments then emerged, such as the popular Warner's 'Merry Widow' collection, which included corselettes and cinch-bras (Figure 1.3). While similar to the early corselette designs of the 1930s, the new styles differed in some fundamental ways. They were shorter in length and included underwire bra cups, waist stays, spiral steel boning and detachable shoulder straps. Their construction from a combination of stretch and lighter-weight woven fabrics provided a new level of comfort.

In the following decades, development in textile technology, garment design and societal changes led to an increase in desire for comfortable and flexible undergarments. Separate bras and panties remained popular for youthful figures, while the corselette continued

Figure 1.3 Warner's 'Merry Widow' corselette that became popular in the 1950s. Promoted as creating an hourglass silhouette, it had a mix of stretch and non-stretch panels, nine spiral steel bones for structure and support, and underwire bra cups. The adjustable closure is located in the back and has sixteen hooks and eyes (author's collection).

to evolve to remain relevant. Constructed from stretch fabrics with varying degrees of compression, modern versions of the corselette no longer relied on rigid fabrics, boning and metal closures. As the corset evolved into the lighter, more flexible corselette, the corselette has itself evolved into a garment offering shaping and control combined with a high level of comfort – shapewear.

Inner corselette designs

The term 'inner corselette' is often used to reference the foundations that were built into Dior gowns to create the wasp waist and uplifted bustline. These inner corselettes were typically hip length with eight panels. Extra shaping was achieved with horizontal darts around the bust and vertical darts through the torso. Boning was added on all seams and sometimes over vertical darts and alongside the closure. The corselette had its own fastening, a zipper or hooks and eyes, allowing it to be more closely fitted than the outer garment, to provide a firm understructure.

Modern dressmaking patterns that include a separate boned understructure refer to them as a foundation or underbodice. They typically have simplified style lines, excluding extra dart shaping, for example. They finish at the waist, preventing any waist reduction or shaping of the figure. While the concept is similar to the inner corselette in that it supports the gown and smooths the upper torso, the design does not have the same ability to shape the figure as a true corselette would. However, a princess-seamed pattern can be adapted to create a more form-fitting foundation, similar to earlier designs.

The inner corselette designs in this book are based on an eight-panelled princess-seamed bodice. Some were included with the pattern, while others were developed from the dress pattern itself. You'll learn how to adapt the basic pattern to include extra dart shaping at the bust and waist to achieve a very form-fitting garment. The designs do not include figure shaping (such as waist cinching or uplifting of the bust) as this involves specific knowledge and techniques which are not addressed here.

Do I need to wear a bra with an inner corselette?

Many inner corselette or foundation designs are based on a princess-seamed bodice and do not include cups, unlike the early corselette. Generally, this design will provide only light support for the breasts and so it is recommended that a bra is worn to provide shape and support. Padded bra cups can be included to add volume to the bustline and smooth the outward appearance, but they do not lift or separate the breasts.

When should I use an inner corselette?

Inner corselettes are commonly associated with bridal and evening wear, but they can be incorporated into a variety of designs. In general, when a garment needs boning in the bodice, you could think about creating an inner corselette to house the necessary support. There are several advantages of incorporating an inner corselette in a garment instead of placing the boning directly into the bodice:

- It allows more freedom for the outer design. Designs with draping, with intricate seam details or which are a looser fit often don't have suitable seamlines for boning to be installed, but require support all the same. An inner corselette provides the structure required to support the outer design.
- A boned bodice must be a snug fit for the boning to be effective. Some fashion fabrics are too delicate or lightweight for a close-fitting silhouette and require added support and ease to gracefully skim over the body. An inner corselette anchored firmly to the figure provides this support while taking the strain off the outer fabrics.
- Many gowns have multiple layers of fabric (lace, fashion fabric, underlining and lining) that can create bulk when inserting a zipper or other type of fastening. By housing the necessary support in a separate garment with its own closure, less fabric is handled at one time.
- It can provide light shaping of the figure.
- It can create a firm structure for attaching skirt linings, ruffles, stiffening and petticoats.

The designs shown in this book are a starting point. Once you have mastered the techniques, you will find many opportunities to apply your skills.

- **Bridal gowns and evening wear.** A close-fitting inner corselette is perfect for providing the necessary structure and support for the delicate fabrics, heavy skirts and embellishments.
- **1950s-style dresses and gowns.** Create a waist- or hip-length inner corselette and attach petticoats of organza, tulle or netting in single or multiple layers to create the desired volume. For added volume and a true vintage silhouette, hem the petticoats with horsehair trim.
- **Costumes.** Incorporate an inner corselette into costumes to provide structural support and achieve the desired silhouette.
- **Bustiers.** Create bodices with interesting seamlines and outer details by incorporating the support in a princess-seamed inner corselette.
- **Off-the-shoulder gowns and jackets.** Anchor this essentially strapless design to the body with an inner corselette to ensure that the bodice stays in place while allowing the arms to move freely.
- **Bodices inspired by architecture.** Have fun with a design that incorporates 3-D shapes and sculptural elements, all cleverly supported by an inner corselette that is hidden beneath.
- **Draped bodices.** Build your inner corselette then drape it in soft gathers, ruching or pleats of chiffon, fine lace or tulle for an ethereal effect.

From casual to formal, classic to dramatic, an inner corselette is the perfect foundation for creating a beautifully engineered bodice.

Anatomy of an inner corselette

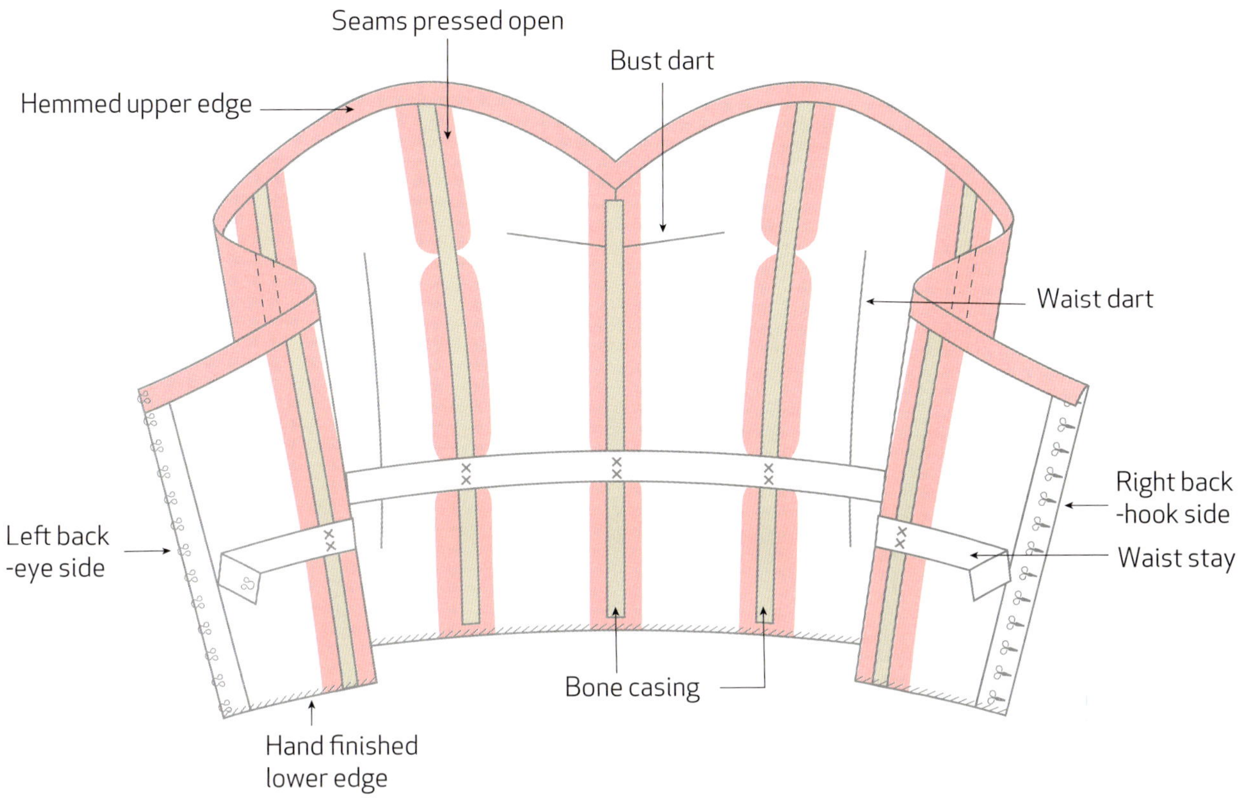

Snug fit
Corselettes fit the body very closely and may be slightly smaller than the body at the waist, to shape the figure.

Multiple seams and darts
Allow for multiple options to refine the fit and shape.

Seams
Seams are typically pressed open.

Strapless
Inner corselettes are usually strapless, although straps may be added to help support a neckline.

Boning
Boning is typically located on the seams and sometimes in the centre of panels.

Waist stay
The waist stay anchors the corselette to the body and takes some tension from the garment closure.

Closure
Inner corselettes can have a zipper or hook-and-eye closure.

Length
An inner corselette finishes either at the waist or at high hip.

2

Selecting and Fitting the Pattern

To create a truly custom corselette with a comfortable, supportive and flattering fit, alterations to a commercial pattern are almost always required. These patterns are drafted to standardized measurements and, for most sewers, a commercial pattern is just a starting point for developing a pattern that fits well. In this section we will explore how a pattern relates to your figure and to the fit of the corselette. This will allow you to select the right pattern size and identify some key initial pattern adjustments you'll need to make before creating a toile. Becoming skilled at fitting takes experience and usually involves much trial and error, but following these steps will make the process easier.

Selecting the pattern

When it comes to selecting the pattern for an inner corselette, there are several options. Both special occasion and day wear patterns can be suitable and it is not essential that separate pattern pieces for a foundation are included. There are three important features to look for in a pattern: it should have minimal ease in the bust (no more than 5cm (2") is ideal); it should be for a woven fabric; and it should have princess seams. While some corselette designs have separate cups, many use a simpler princess-seamed bodice that is easier to sew and fit. Here we'll discuss three options for selecting a corselette pattern from easiest to most challenging.

The simplest way to begin is to choose a pattern that includes a separate boned foundation or underbodice. Most often, this will be a bridal or evening wear design. The hard work of designing the corselette to match the outer design is already done and the focus can be on fit and construction. You can decide whether to follow the construction steps provided with the pattern, or incorporate your preferred methods.

Beginning with a pattern for a strapless gown is another option. The pattern is simply traced from the upper edge to the waist or hips to create the corselette pattern. Alternatively, the lining pattern may be suitable to use if the bodice of the gown does not have princess seams. During the toile fitting, the corselette fit is adjusted to create a form-fitting foundation. In this approach, the corselette shares the same upper edge and proportions as the outer garment, ensuring that they will fit together well.

The most challenging method for developing a corselette pattern is to begin with a pattern for a princess-seamed sheath. A customized block can also be used, in which case the darts should be converted to princess seams. A few more steps are involved to tighten the design and remove the shoulder area, and more than one toile will likely be needed. The modified pattern is then used to build the corselette and create the pattern for the outer garment.

Measuring for a corselette

In order to choose the correct pattern size, you must first take a set of accurate body measurements. While the pattern size will be chosen based on the bust measurement, other measurements are important for making some preliminary adjustments to a corselette pattern. Body measurements can be affected by posture and the undergarments worn, so it is important to take the time to properly prepare for the measuring session. If measuring yourself, having a measuring buddy will make the process easier. A 'Personal fitting worksheet' for you to record your measurements on and calculate your pattern ease and adjustments is included at the end of this chapter (see page 21).

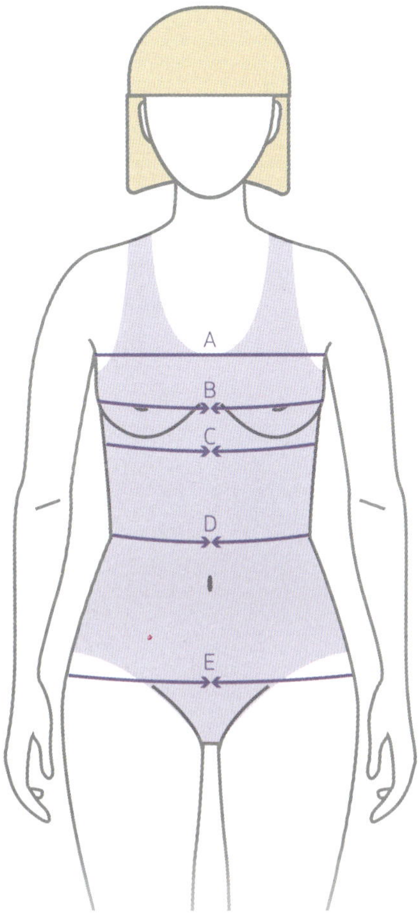

Figure 2.1

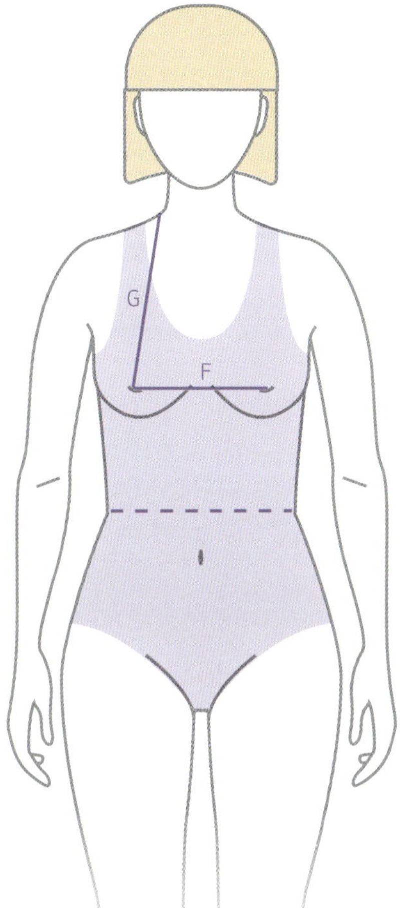

Figure 2.2

A. Front width
The distance between the two armhole creases, keeping the tape measure parallel to the floor. Take the measurement flat; do not wrap the tape measure over the body curves or into the underarm area.

B. Full bust
Measure around the body over the fullest part of the bust, keeping the tape measure parallel to the floor.

C. Underbust
Measure around the body directly under the bust, keeping the tape measure parallel to the floor.

D. Waist
Measure directly over the elastic placed at the waistline.

E. Hip
Measure the widest part of the lower body approximately 20cm–22cm (8"–9") below the waist. With the tape measure parallel to the floor, wiggle the tape measure down until you find the widest point.

F. Bust width
Measure from apex to apex, keeping the tape measure parallel to the floor. If measuring another person, hold the tape just away from the body.

G. Bust depth
The distance from the base of the neck at the shoulder, to the bust apex.

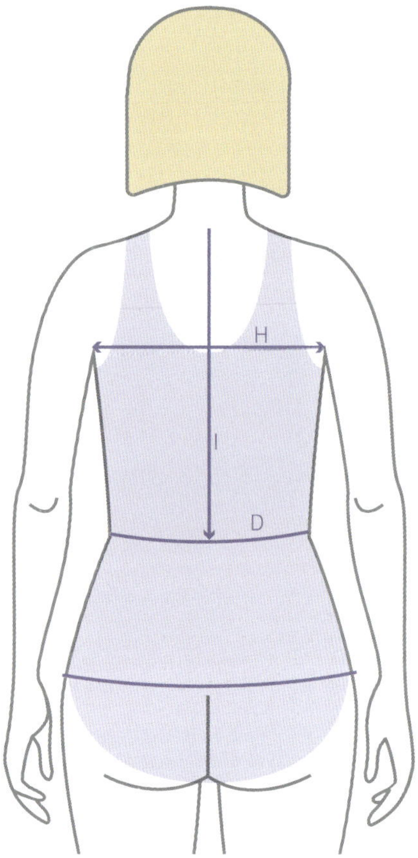

Figure 2.3

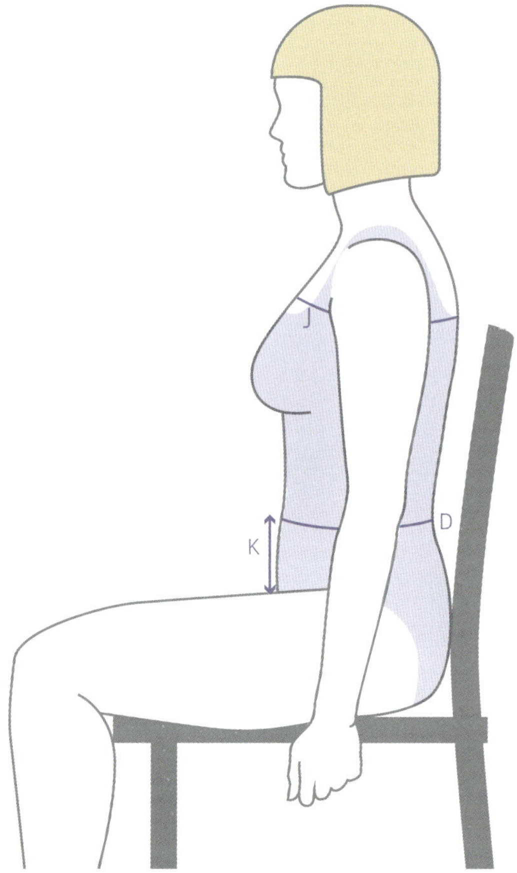

Figure 2.4

H. Back width
Measure between the two armhole creases. Take the measurement flat across the back keeping the tape measure parallel to the floor.

I. Back length
Measure from the base of the neck to the bottom of the waist elastic. To find the base of the neck, tilt the head slightly forward and locate the vertebra that protrudes. Straighten before taking the measurement.

J. High bust
Measure around the body at underarm level, keeping the tape measure parallel to the floor at the back, angling it under the arm and across the top of the bust at the front.

K. Lap length
When seated, measure from the bottom of the waist elastic to the top of the thigh in line with the centre of the breast, keeping the tape measure taut (this is the maximum length for a corselette).

Preparing for a measuring session

- Wear a well-fitting bra, ideally the one that will be worn under the final garment. The bra will affect the measurements of the bust height, shape and fullness.
- Wear close-fitting but not constricting clothes. If you are measuring in private, wear only your bra and underwear or, for modesty, wear a camisole or slip.
- Tie up long hair.
- Wear a fine chain to identify the base of the neck.
- Tie a narrow piece of elastic around your waist.
- Wear flat shoes or bare feet.
- Stand as naturally as possible. Keep your arms relaxed and do not pull in your stomach or stand extra straight.
- Stand in front of a full-length mirror if possible.

Tips for measuring

- Place a length of narrow elastic around the waistline and tie it so that it is snug but not tight. To find your waistline, gently lean to one side and note where your body bends. This is your natural waistline.
- When measuring a circumference, always keep the tape measure parallel to the floor.
- Record the exact measurement; do not add ease.
- Measure to the nearest 1cm or ½". Due to natural weight fluctuations, this is accurate enough.

Selecting the pattern size

Size charts are provided on the back of the pattern envelope to indicate the best size for your personal measurements. Remember that this is just a starting point. There will be some preliminary adjustments made to the paper pattern and then further alterations can be made during the fitting of the toile.

For a corselette, the pattern size is chosen based on your bust measurement, but for greater accuracy your cup size should also be considered. This will help you choose the pattern size that is appropriate for your frame, providing a better fit through the shoulders, chest and upper back. A small bust or full bust adjustment can then be made to achieve a better fit through the bust.

Finding your cup size

Cup size is the difference between the full bust and the high bust measurement. Some patterns come with a range of cup sizes; however, the majority of commercial patterns are drafted for a B cup and a bust cup adjustment is necessary for other cup sizes. Independent pattern company websites often state the cup size of their patterns, so try to locate this information, if possible. Use Table 1 to determine your cup size.

Table 1 Cup sizes

FULL BUST – HIGH BUST = CUP SIZE	
A cup:	difference of 2.5cm (1") or less
B cup:	difference of 2.5cm–5cm (1"–2")
C cup:	difference of 5cm–7.5cm (2"–3")
D cup:	difference of 7.5cm–10cm (3"–4")
DD/E cup:	difference of 10cm–12.5cm (4"–5")
EE/F cup:	difference of 12.5cm–15cm (5"–6")
G cup:	difference of 15cm–17.5cm (6"–7")
H cup:	difference of 17.5cm–20cm (7"–8")

Choosing the correct pattern size

Compare your cup size to that of the pattern. This will tell you if you should choose your pattern size based on your full bust measurement or your high bust measurement.

- If your cup size is the same as the cup size the pattern was designed for then select the pattern size according to your full bust measurement.
- If your cup size is different from that of the pattern, it is best to choose the pattern size based on your high bust measurement and then make an adjustment to the cup size. In this way you will select a pattern size that fits your frame better and requires fewer alterations.

Most patterns are drafted for a B cup, where the full bust measurement is 5cm (2") larger than the high bust measurement. This means that if you add 5cm (2") to your high bust measurement, you will know what your full bust measurement would be if you were a B cup. Using this measurement, select the recommended pattern size from the size chart on the pattern envelope, then make a small bust or full bust adjustment to improve the fit through the bust.

Let's look at an example where you are a D cup, and the pattern is drafted for a B cup.

1. Begin with your high bust measurement and add 5cm (2").
2. Compare this measurement to the bust measurements given in the size chart on the back of the pattern envelope. Select the pattern size that is closest to this measurement.
3. Make a full bust adjustment to increase the B cup of the pattern to match your D cup.

- If your pattern includes multiple cup sizes, use your high bust measurement to select the pattern size as described, then select the pattern pieces for your cup size. If your cup size is larger than those provided with the pattern, select the largest size available then make a full bust adjustment to add the additional amount necessary.

TIP

If your bust measurement falls between sizes, it is usually best to choose the smaller size.

TIP

When making a full bust or small bust adjustment, divide the total amount of the required adjustment in half. As the front pattern pieces are cut in pairs or on the fold, the adjustment is made to the pattern for one side of the body only. The amount added or subtracted from the pattern during the adjustment will be doubled across the full width of the front bodice.

TIP

If the pattern has been designed for a C cup, you will use your high bust measurement plus 7.5cm (3"). This would be your full bust measurement if you were a C cup.

Understanding ease

The amount of ease in a pattern is the difference between the pattern measurement and the corresponding body measurement. Knowing the amount of ease in a pattern will guide you in predicting the fit of the garment for your figure and identifying areas of the pattern that may need to be adjusted.

There are several types of ease:

- **Wearing ease** refers to the minimum amount of extra length or width that must be added to the body measurements to allow movement while wearing the garment. This is what gives enough room to move and to comfortably perform day-to-day activities. The amount of minimal wearing ease is affected by the type of garment and the fabric choice, as well as personal comfort.
- **Design ease** refers to the extra volume built into a pattern for style purposes. This is additional to the wearing ease and is used to create style elements such as loose-fitting tops, gathered sleeves and full skirts.
- **Negative ease** refers to the pattern being smaller than the body measurements and the fit depending upon the garment stretching and hugging the body. It is generally seen in patterns that use stretch-knit fabrics, but also is how a waist reduction is achieved in a corset or corselette. If the corselette is intended to cinch the waist, the pattern measurement at the waistline will be smaller than the body measurement, perhaps by 2.5cm–5cm (1"–2").

Corselette ease

To achieve the desired close fit of an inner corselette, the finished garment should have little to no wearing ease. Generally, there is no ease at the waist and less than 2.5cm (1") at the bust and hips, allowing for boning. The outer garment will often have more ease than your corselette, but it is important that at the points where the corselette and the outer garment connect, the measurements are the same.

Determining pattern ease

To determine the amount of ease in the pattern, you will need to find the finished pattern measurements so that you can compare them to your personal measurements. This will let you know which areas of the pattern may need adjusting to achieve a better fit. The pattern ease will then be adjusted before cutting your toile.

Pattern measurement − Personal measurement = Ease

Key points for comparison are the bust, waist and hip circumferences as well as the back length. The bust depth is also useful to know, but it can be more difficult to determine in a pattern for a strapless garment. Often, the finished measurements for the bust, waist and hip are marked on the pattern. If they are not, you can measure the circumference of the pattern at each of these points (Figure 2.5). The 'depth below base of neck' measurement is often stated on the centre back pattern piece and can be added to the pattern measurement to determine the total back length to the waist. Alternatively, the back waist length for each pattern size can usually be found in the Body Measurements table on the pattern instructions.

It's best to start with a pattern that has 4cm–5cm (1¾"–2") of ease above your personal measurements, to allow space for the boning, closures and lining. Any extra ease can be removed during the toile fitting to customize the fit. Compare the finished pattern measurements to your personal measurements at each of the key points. Note the amount of ease at each point and where the pattern may need to be enlarged or reduced to achieve the ideal amount of starting ease. In addition, note any lengthwise adjustments necessary, for example changes to the back length or bust height (see Table 2).

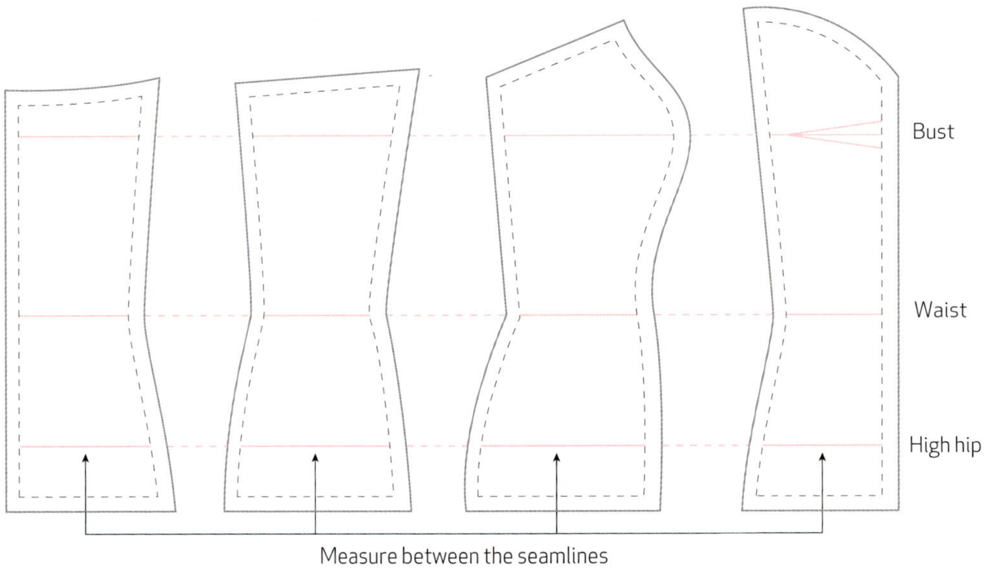

Figure 2.5

Table 2 Example – Adjusting pattern ease

	FINISHED PATTERN MEASUREMENT	BODY MEASUREMENT	EASE	ADJUSTMENT TO PATTERN
Bust	98cm (38½")	94cm (37")	+4cm (1½")	No change
Waist	77cm (30¼")	79cm (31")	-2cm (¾")	Increase waist circumference
Hips	102cm (40")	95cm (37½")	+7cm (2¾")	Reduce hip circumference
Back waist	42.5cm (16¾")	40cm (15¾")	+2.5cm (1")	Reduce length above waist

Adjusting the pattern

Once you have calculated the pattern ease, some initial adjustments for your body can be completed before cutting the toile, reducing the need for alterations during the toile fitting. This is when you can adjust the pattern length, cup size and circumferences to better match your body shape and proportions.

Begin by calculating the amount by which each pattern circumference measurement needs to be adjusted to achieve the desired amount of starting ease. As you are working with half the pattern, you will halve each measurement and this will be the amount you will add to or remove from the pattern. When adjusting the pattern, small changes can often be made in the side seams; however, if larger amounts need to be added or subtracted, it's best to spread that amount over all the seams or by adding waist darts.

Making the adjustments

1. Mark all seamlines onto the traced pattern. Adjustments are made on, or within, these lines, not the cut edge.
2. Make lengthwise adjustments first, followed by bust cup adjustments then circumference changes, using your preferred alteration method. Adjusting the cup size will affect the waist and hip measurements of the pattern, so it is important to re-measure these after the cup adjustment is completed and to update the amount of change needed.
3. If desired, add a dart at the centre front at bust level, to bring the corselette closer to the chest (Figure 2.6).
4. Once the adjustments are complete, true the pattern (see below). Straighten the grainlines if necessary (they should be perpendicular to the waist or hip line) and increase the seam allowances to 2.5cm (1"). This gives some room for adjustments during the fitting stage.
5. Mark the desired length of the corselette, finishing it either at the waist or between the waist and your lap length measurement.
6. To keep the seamlines free for alterations, mark a temporary boning placement line in the centre of each.

Truing the pattern

Blend and smooth any seamlines that have been altered. Compare each seam with the one it will be sewn to, checking that they are the same length and that notches match. Adjust the seams if necessary, so that they are of equal length. Check that there is a smooth transition across seams at the neckline, shoulders, armholes and lower edges.

Waist length or hip length?

Many foundation or corselette designs finish at the waistline, which is sufficient to smooth the upper body and support the bodice. However, extending it down to the hip has several advantages:

- The boning is more comfortable when extended and avoids the potential of it digging in at the waist.
- It gives a smoother shape below the waist. A tight garment ending at the waistline can cause a small pooch below it on all but the slimmest of figures.
- If desired, it can allow for cinching of the waist.
- It can be used to anchor underskirts or petticoats lower on the torso, keeping the waistline free from added bulk.

Adding a centre front dart

It is common for an inner corselette to have a dart sewn at bust level at the centre front; this is sometimes called a 'Hollywood' dart. This shaping brings the centre front closer to the sternum and helps give a snugger fit around the bust. Using a centre front seam will give the best result, allowing the fit to be better adjusted. During the fitting of the toile, the fit can be refined to suit your body shape and cup size; you can adjust the upper edge, if necessary, to maintain its original shape and height. A small amount of width may need to be added at bust level to allow the corselette to reach the sternum.

Adding the dart

1. Mark the seam allowances on the centre front panel.
2. Draw a line perpendicular to the centre front to the bust point, then mark 8mm (5/16") either side of the line at the centre front.
3. Measure in 1.5cm (5/8") from the bust point and mark the end of the dart. From this point, draw the dart legs back to the opening at the centre front (Figure 2.6).
4. True the dart legs and add a seam at the centre front.

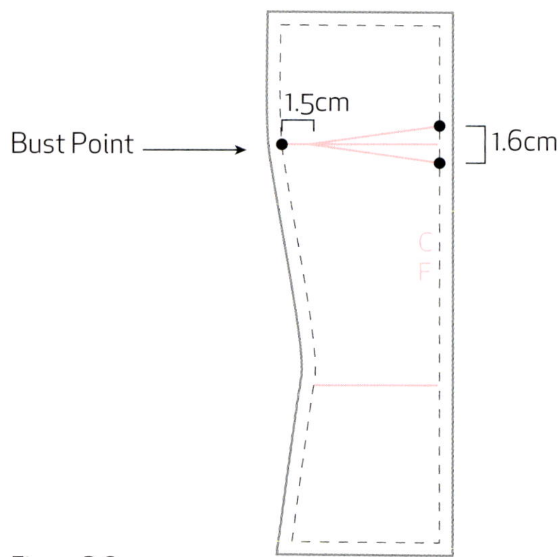

Figure 2.6

Personal fitting worksheet for an inner corselette

	PERSONAL MEASUREMENT	PATTERN MEASUREMENT	AMOUNT OF PATTERN EASE	PATTERN ADJUSTMENT NEEDED
Front width				
High bust				
Full bust				
Underbust				
Waist				
Hip				
Bust width				
Bust depth				
Back width				
Back length				
Lap length				

Cup size

__________ – __________ = __________

(Full Bust) (High Bust) (Cup size)

Difference	Cup size
2.5cm (1") or less	A
2.5cm–5cm (1"–2")	B
5cm–7.5cm (2"–3")	C
7.5cm–10cm (3"–4")	D
10cm–12.5cm (4"–5")	DD/E
12.5cm–15cm (5"–6")	EE/F
15cm–17.5cm (6"–7")	G
17.5cm–20cm (7"–8")	H

Selecting the pattern size

Personal cup size = Pattern cup size	Choose the pattern size using your full bust measurement.
Personal cup size < Pattern cup size	Choose the pattern size using your high bust measurement and make a small bust adjustment.
Personal cup size > Pattern cup size	Choose the pattern size using your high bust measurement and make a full bust adjustment.

3

Making the Toile

A toile, sometimes referred to as a muslin or mock-up, is an important step in creating a well-fitted garment. It is essentially a trial run of the garment that allows the design, assembly and fit to be tested and perfected before cutting the fashion fabric. For best results, a toile should be made for both the corselette and the outer garment. This allows them to be layered as they will be worn, enabling a true assessment of the fit and design. You can check details such as if the corselette upper edge is visible, if the boning placement is adequate and if match points correspond correctly. Sometimes several toiles may be needed before you are satisfied with the fit, but the benefits are well worth the effort.

Once your initial pattern adjustments are completed, you are ready to prepare the toiles. Ensure that all the preliminary adjustments made to the corselette pattern are transferred to the pattern for the outer garment, such as changes to the length or circumference, cup size adjustments and alterations to the style line along the upper edge. Compare both patterns to make a final check that all match points and placement lines correspond.

Calico is a good choice for making the corselette toile. For the outer garment, choose a toile fabric that has similar characteristics to the fashion fabric that will be used. Follow the same process used to construct the corselette toile, but it's not necessary to add all the details. Only assemble the main pattern pieces needed to assess the fit and design. Facings and pockets can be eliminated, while collars and cuffs can be attached as a single layer to check their proportion and fit. For a one-piece dress or gown, a toile of the whole design is usually required. A toile of the bodice and the sleeves only may be sufficient for a two-piece design where the skirt has a lot of fullness.

Constructing the toile

Even though your corselette may have two layers, your toile can be made from a single layer of sturdy, non-stretch fabric such as calico or muslin. Press the fabric to remove creases then fold it in half lengthwise.

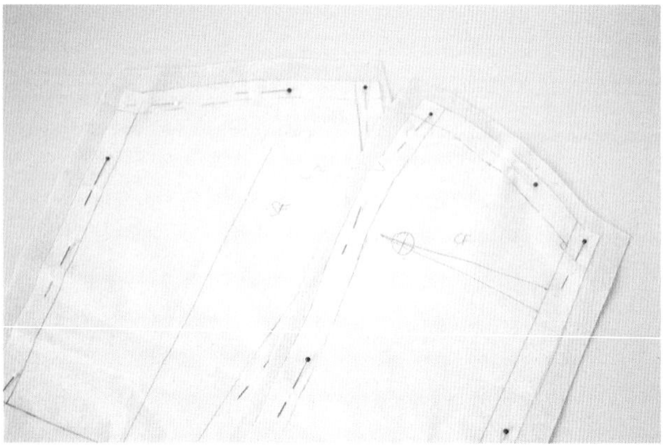

Figure 3.1

Cut the pattern

1. Lay out the pattern pieces and secure. Cut out each piece, leaving a generous allowance (3cm–4cm or 1¼"–1½") at the upper and lower edges so that the shape can be refined on the body. Allow 2.5cm (1") minimum on all other seams for adjustments during the fitting (Figure 3.1).

Transfer the pattern markings

1. With the two layers of fabric still attached to the pattern, lay them fabric-side down on a sheet of waxed tracing paper (Figure 3.2). Using a tracing wheel, transfer the following information from the paper pattern onto the lower fabric layer:
   - All seamlines and darts.
   - Temporary bone placement.
   - Upper and lower edges.
   - Notches and grainlines.
   - Waistline, bust apex and any other information that may be pertinent to the design.

Figure 3.2

2. Remove the paper pattern then re-pin the two fabric pieces together, taking care not to shift them. Turn the pieces over, placing the opposite fabric side on the waxed tracing paper. Trace over the first set of marks to transfer them onto the lower fabric layer (Figure 3.3).
3. Label each pattern piece. This avoids confusing them, as they may be difficult to tell apart.

Figure 3.3

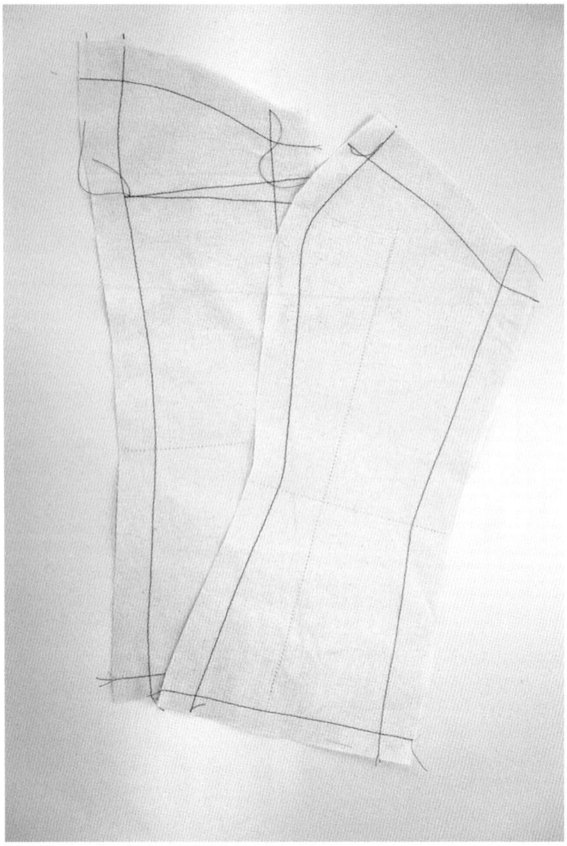

Figure 3.4

Thread trace the seamlines

When all pieces are marked, use a dark thread to machine baste all stitching lines. As the stitching can be seen from both sides, it makes it easier to match the seams for pinning and sewing. It also gives a clear guideline when marking and making alterations. It is important to sew each line separately, stitching to the edges of the fabric rather than pivoting at the corners. Stitch each dart leg separately also, extending each line beyond the dart point (Figure 3.4).

Baste the panels

Using a different-coloured thread and a long stitch length, machine baste the toile together. As your corselette will be a very snug fit, machine basting is better than hand basting. First sew the darts, then sew each seam from edge to edge. Be sure to stitch exactly on the thread traced seamlines.

Figure 3.5

Add the boning

You will need to place boning into your toile to properly assess the fit of your corselette. Although your corselette will likely have boning on the seamlines, it is helpful to place the boning close to the seamline or in the centre of the panel on the toile, to make adjustments easier. You can use sew-in boning or add casings and boning which can be removed for use in your actual corselette. Baste the boning in place. If you are fitting yourself, a zipper basted in the opening seam will be helpful. If you are using bust padding, also baste it in place (Figure 3.5).

Fitting the toile

Once you have assembled your toile, it is ready for the first fitting. Be sure to have the following tools handy:

- Tape measure.
- Seam ripper.
- Pen or pencil.
- Pins.
- Scraps of the toile fabric.

Ideally, conduct the fitting in front of a full-length mirror, tie up long hair and wear the undergarments that will be worn with the final garment. Some people like to take photos during the fitting, particularly of difficult-to-reach areas like the back.

Before making any changes to your toile, assess it as a whole. Check that the toile is positioned correctly on your body and whether it feels comfortable. Do any areas feel too tight or too loose? Is the upper edge the correct height and shape, and does the lower edge dig into your lap when you're sitting? Use the 'Assessing the fit' checklist to determine what alterations may be needed.

If a large number of alterations are needed, it is better to start with the more substantial changes in the first fitting and then transfer the alterations to the toile for a second fitting. Sometimes it can be better to make a new toile and continue the adjustments in a second fitting session. Keep in mind that it's likely that you will need extra toile fittings if the design is complex or if there are a number of fitting challenges.

Assessing the fit

- The corselette should be snug through the waist and torso but not dig in anywhere.
- The upper edge should not sit away from the body, nor should it be too tight, creating spillage at the back or front.
- The lower edge should be a close fit but allow enough room for movement.
- The corselette waistline should sit at the natural waistline.
- The bust guideline should match the bust level on the figure.
- Horizontal darts should point to the fullest part of the bust.
- Princess seams should pass over the centre of the bust.
- The underbust area should be snug against the ribcage.
- If centre front horizontal darts are used, the centre front should lie close to the sternum.
- Bust padding should be centred over the bust apex.
- The side seams should sit at the side of the body and be perpendicular to the floor.
- The side length should be a comfortable distance from the armpit.
- Grainlines should be perpendicular to the floor.
- When seated, the sides should not be so high that the boning digs into the armpits and the lower edge should finish above the hip bone.

Adjusting the toile

Once you have assessed the toile as a whole, you are ready to begin making the adjustments (Figure 3.6).

Figure 3.6

1. Make lengthwise adjustments first so that the bust, waist and hips of the toile match those points on the body.
2. Adjust the circumference, matching the contours of the body. Pinning changes in small increments over multiple areas will usually give a better fit than adding or subtracting a large amount in one or two places. Check the depth and position of the bust dart if applicable.
3. Mark the height and shape of the upper edge, then mark the lower edge, ensuring that it doesn't dig into the lap when seated.
4. Check the position of the bust padding if it is being used and adjust if necessary.
5. Assess the boning placement. Determine the amount and placement of boning required (see Chapter 7 for boning layout).
6. Add the waist stay, positioning the lower edge on the natural waistline. Mark the waistline on the toile along the lower edge of the waist stay.

Marking the changes

Once you are happy with the fit, you will need to mark the adjustments on the toile (Figure 3.7). I also like to transfer them to the paper pattern.

1. On the toile, mark all the adjustments made. If a seamline has been altered, draw its new placement, add or adjust darts as necessary and mark any changes to the upper and lower edges.
2. Transfer all changes to the paper pattern. Blend the new seam markings and edges, ensuring smooth transitions and design lines.
3. True all darts and stitching lines.

If necessary, make another toile and repeat the process. While further fittings will occur in the fashion fabric, by the end of the toile phase most of the major fitting issues should have been addressed and resolved.

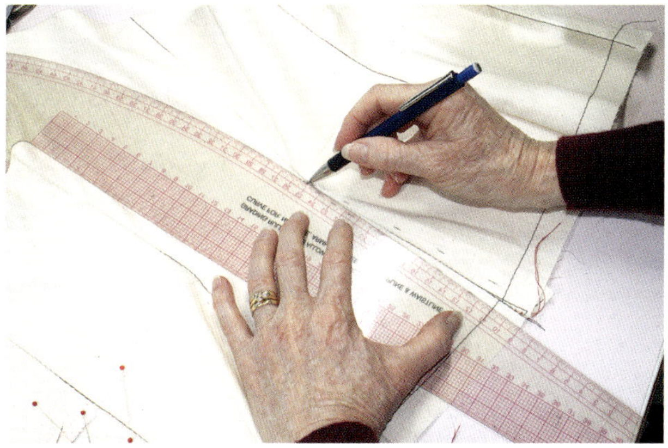

Figure 3.7

4

Selecting Fabrics, Notions and Boning

There are many elements used to build a corselette – many of which you will be familiar with from other sewing projects. Along with selecting a fashion fabric you will need to consider tapes, ribbons and bone casings, as well as the types of boning and fasteners that best suit your project. Your selections will be influenced by how much support is required by the outer garment, the figure of the wearer and the amount of wear the garment will receive. Of course, personal preferences, availability of resources and budget will influence these choices as well. Experimenting with different combinations of fabrics and notions is the ideal way to learn which elements work best for you and for each individual project.

Figure 4.1

Fabrics

There are several important things to consider when choosing the right fabric for your corselette. Many demands are placed on corselettes because they are snug-fitting and worn next to the skin. The fabric needs to be sturdy but lightweight, breathable, absorbent and comfortable and it must perform well under tension. Plain weave natural fibres are best, with cotton and silk the most popular choices (Figure 4.1). Below is a list of suggested fabrics, each suitable for a range of different projects.

Cottons

Cotton fabrics are readily available, generally well-priced, easy to sew, comfortable and absorbent. They are a good base for a corselette and an ideal choice for the first project. They are frequently sewn with two layers on opposite grains for extra strength and stability. Heavier weights (drill, broadcloth and coutil) may be strong enough in a single layer. There are a variety of cotton fabrics that are suitable.

Poplin

Poplin is a plain weave, tightly woven, medium-weight fabric with a subtle crosswise rib. Known for its durability and lustre, poplin is readily available, relatively inexpensive and comes in a variety of colours. It's commonly found in cotton and cotton blends, and it should be pre-washed prior to cutting to remove shrinkage.

Calico

Calico is a plain weave cotton, commonly used for toiles (muslins), soft home furnishings, crafts and curtains. It is a well-priced, sturdy and durable fabric, and a good-quality (smooth) calico can be suitable for a dress foundation. Calico should be pre-washed prior to cutting to remove shrinkage.

Drill

Drill is a sturdy, medium-weight fabric, usually made of cotton or cotton blends. It has a tight diagonal (twill) weave and can be found in a variety of colours. Drill should be pre-washed prior to cutting to remove shrinkage.

Broadcloth

Broadcloth is a medium to heavyweight, tightly woven, plain weave fabric with a subtle rib. It's usually made of cotton or cotton blends, is readily available and comes in a range of colours. Broadcloth should be pre-washed prior to cutting.

Coutil

Coutil is a tightly woven, strong and durable fabric originally designed for corsetry. Coutil usually has a high cotton content and comes in a variety of weights, weaves (herringbone, satin and brocade) and colours. It is more expensive than other options and available only from specialized retailers; however, its strength and durability make it suitable for figures where more support is desired or for body shaping garments. To remove shrinkage, coutil can be pre-washed, though washing will soften it. Alternatively, steaming it prior to cutting will maintain its crispness while dealing with any shrinkage.

Linen

Pure linen is a crisp, strong fabric. It is comfortable, absorbent and available in a variety of colours, textures and weights. Prices will vary according to the type and quality. For a corselette, it's best to choose a medium-weight linen with a smooth texture and to use two layers cut on opposite grains for stability. Linen should be pre-washed prior to cutting to remove shrinkage.

Silks

Overall, silk fabrics are more expensive than cotton and they require more care when sewing to achieve smooth, pucker-free seams. Pins and stitching also have a tendency to leave permanent marks, so alterations should be kept to a minimum. Bearing all this in mind, silk fabrics are probably better suited to a more experienced sewer. Silks have a smooth surface, allowing them to work well under a variety of outer fabrics, as the garment glides over the corselette. The silk fabrics most often used for a corselette are organza and taffeta.

Silk organza

Organza is a plain weave, lightweight, sheer fabric with a crisp hand and is quite strong for its weight. Traditionally made from silk, organza is now also found in synthetics, which are less comfortable in a close-fitting garment. Silk organza comes in a wide variety of colours and can also be found printed and embroidered. It should be well steamed prior to cutting. Washing should be avoided as the organza will soften.

Silk taffeta

Taffeta is a strong, crisp, plain weave fabric with a shiny, smooth surface and is available in a range of weights. Originally woven from silk, it now comes in both synthetic and silk varieties that are available in a wide range of colours. Choose a mid-weight taffeta and use two layers cut on opposite grains to give a stronger finish. The fabric unravels easily, so plan to finish or enclose the seam allowances. Taffeta should be steamed prior to cutting to remove shrinkage.

Bobbinet

Bobbinet, also called genuine or Swiss tulle, is stable, lightweight and noted for being exceptionally strong for its weight. It is available in cotton, silk and synthetics. It is more expensive and available only through specialized retailers. This mesh fabric uses different techniques for cutting and sewing, requiring more experience; however, it is easy to handle. If the finished garment will be hand-washed, cotton bobbinet should be pre-washed prior to cutting, as it will shrink. Silk bobbinet should be well steamed. A bobbinet corselette traditionally consists of two layers cut on opposite grains.

Boning

Stiffening of fabrics has been used for centuries to shape the body into a fashionable silhouette. It can be applied to bodices and skirts to create a smooth base, to structure a garment or to mould the body itself.

Boning is usually associated with strapless evening gowns and corsets. It can also be used to hold the shape of hooped petticoats, as well as to add light support for details such as midriffs and necklines. Originally made from baleen (whalebone), modern boning is made from plastic and metal. There are many types of boning available with different strengths, uses and maintenance needs.

Plastic boning

Plastic boning is readily available and easy to use, making it a popular choice. It comes in a range of strengths and is ideal for areas where light to moderate support is needed. When supporting a fuller bust or a heavy gown, lighter-weight types are generally not strong enough. Most types are also unsuitable for body shaping. There are many types of plastic boning available and it can be found in a range of sizes. Generally, it comes in continuous lengths and is easily cut to the required length with scissors. Plastic boning bends forwards and backwards, not sideways, so it can only be applied in a straight line. Listed below, from lightest to firmest support, are a range of plastic bones.

Woven polyester boning

Made from thin strips of plastic woven together, woven plastic boning is the lightest and most flexible of the bones (Figure 4.2). Available in black, white and clear, it is sold on rolls in widths ranging from 6mm to 13mm (¼"–⅜"). It provides light stiffening for a bodice or design details.

It can be cut to the required length with scissors and the ends covered with a densely woven fabric to prevent the plastic strips from poking out. Alternatively, you can slightly melt the ends by holding them near a candle flame. Plastic end caps are also available, but they will add bulk. Woven polyester boning can be installed in a casing or sewn directly to the fabric. It can also be purchased bonded to a tape or ribbon for easy installation. To uncurl the boning as it comes off the roll, place it under a press cloth and heat with an iron. It can also be lightly moulded and shaped with heat and can be washed or dry cleaned.

Figure 4.2

TIP

When melting the ends of woven polyester boning, work over a sink in a well-ventilated area and take care not to set the boning alight.

Covered boning

Covered boning is a 6mm-wide (¼"-wide) translucent plastic strip with small lengthwise ridges and gives light to moderate support in a bodice. It cannot be sewn through but is sold in a casing ready to use. Covered boning usually comes on rolls and can be purchased by the metre (Figure 4.3).

Gently steam the boning or soak it in warm water to flatten. When cutting a piece to size, use scissors to cut a section 2cm (¾") longer than required, peel the casing back and trim the boning to size and then smooth the ends with an emery board. Next, fold the casing over the bone ends and slipstitch it in place or run the casings to the edge of the garment and catch them in the upper and lower seamlines. Covered boning can be lightly shaped with steam and is washable.

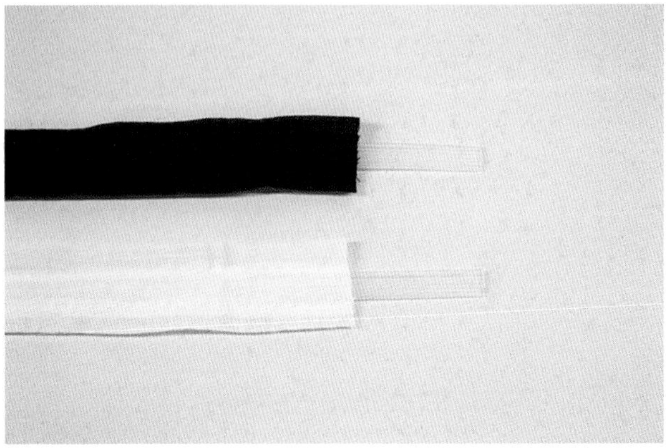

Figure 4.3

Figure 4.4

Figure 4.5

Reinforced (German) plastic boning

Reinforced plastic boning is opaque and has strong lengthwise plastic strips which prevent twisting (Figure 4.4). Available on a continuous roll in several widths from 5mm to 10mm (¼"–⅜"), it offers moderate support in a bodice.

To use, cut pieces to the desired length with scissors and smooth the ends with an emery board. Reinforced boning can be sewn to the fabric or inserted into a casing. To remove the curve from being stored on a roll, soak the bone in hot water or place it under a press cloth and gently heat with an iron. It can be shaped with steam and is washable.

Synthetic whalebone

Smooth, opaque and lightweight, synthetic whalebone offers firm support in a bodice (Figure 4.5). Unlike other types of plastic boning, it will spring back into shape if bent, allowing it to mould and shape the body. It comes in widths from 6mm to 12mm (¼"–⅜") in a regular and a heavy thickness.

Synthetic whalebone comes on a roll and is cut to size with scissors and the ends smoothed with an emery board. It cannot be sewn through so must be placed into a casing. To straighten synthetic whalebone as it comes off the roll, or to mould and shape it, place it under a press cloth and gently heat it with a warm iron. It can be washed or dry cleaned.

Boning is sometimes described as having 'spring'. This means that the bone will return to its original shape if bent or flexed. It is this quality which makes a bone suitable for use in body shaping.

Metal boning

Metal boning comes in several types and is generally stronger than plastic boning. It requires specific tools and skills to cut it to length and finish the ends, so it's also a little more challenging to use. Due to its strength and spring, metal boning is suitable for body shaping or when greater support is required.

Spiral steel boning

Spiral steel boning is exceptionally strong and the most flexible type of boning, bending forwards, backwards and sideways to give optimal levels of movement and comfort for the wearer. Widths range from 5mm to 11mm (¼"–½") and they are sold in pre-cut lengths or on a continuous reel (Figure 4.6). Their flexibility makes them ideal for a corselette, where they are generally used in a 5mm–6mm (¼") width.

The ends of pre-cut lengths are dipped or covered with an end cap. Continuous rolls are cut to the required length with side cutters and the ends are covered with an end cap. Spiral boning must be installed in a casing. It may be dry cleaned.

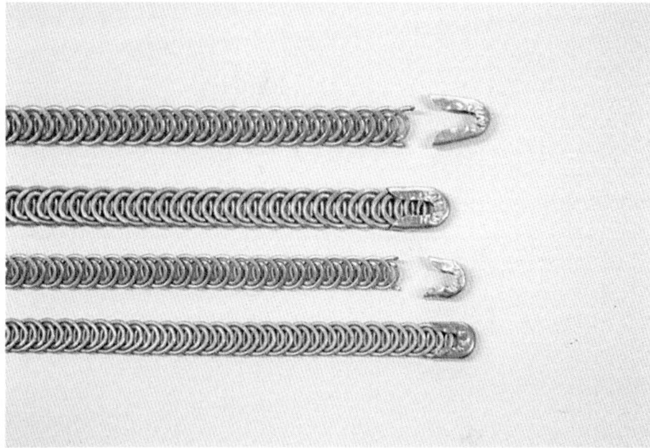

Figure 4.6

Flat (spring) steel boning

Providing extremely strong support, flat steel bones are available in widths ranging from 5mm to 15mm (¼"–⅝") (Figure 4.7). They flex forwards and backwards, but not sideways, so can only be applied in a straight line, but their 'spring' makes them suitable for body shaping. Commonly used in corsetry, these are too rigid for an inner corselette.

Figure 4.7

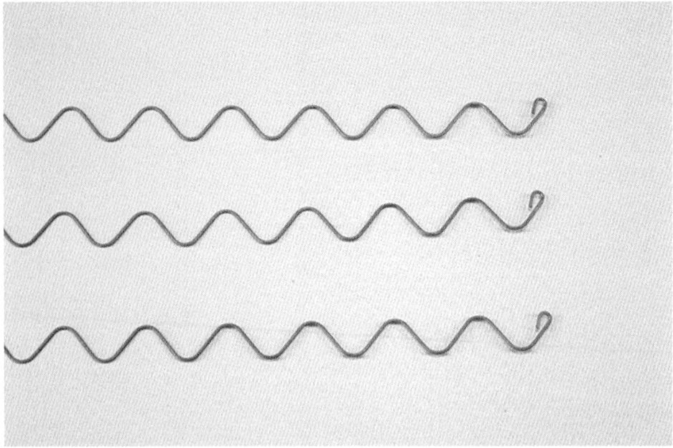

Figure 4.8

Zigzag wires

A less commonly seen type of metal boning is the lighter -weight zigzag wires, also known as 'wiggle bones' (Figure 4.8). Originally used to support high stand-up collars in Edwardian times, these are suitable for areas where lightweight support is required. The wires can be bent, enabling them to hold a desired shape or angle. They are sometimes used to bone the upper part of the front princess seam over the bust curve but are also suitable for holding design elements or providing lightweight support to a neckline. Available in pre-cut lengths, they can be cut to size with wire cutters and the cut ends curled in with pliers. They are stitched to the seam allowance or underlining with an overcast stitch and covered with seam binding or inserted into a casing.

Selecting your boning

There is a role for both plastic and metal bones in garment sewing. Both have the ability to stiffen and support your garment, in varying degrees. To decide which boning is best for your project, consider what you are trying to achieve, both for the garment and for the figure. Is the boning supporting a full or curvaceous figure? Is light support needed to smooth the bodice or control a design detail, or is the boning required to support an embellished strapless gown? How often will the garment be worn and laundered? The more work required of the boning to support the garment or the body, the stronger it needs to be.

Plastic boning is economical and easy to use, but some types provide only light support. If you are supporting a fuller bust, a heavier gown or have light body shaping built into your corselette, choose plastic boning which offers moderate to firm support.

While more expensive and a little more challenging to use and maintain, metal boning is the most supportive and flexible and is suitable for a range of situations. Often more than one type of boning might work for your project, so your decision may depend on personal preference, accessibility or affordability. If you are just beginning with these techniques, good-quality plastic boning is a suitable place to start.

Tapes

A variety of tapes and ribbons are used in the construction of an inner corselette to finish the edges, add strength and stability, and house the boning.

Twill tape

Twill tape has a distinctive herringbone weave and is typically made of cotton (Figure 4.9). It is a sturdy, non-stretch tape and ranges in width from 6mm to 25mm (¼"–1"). Readily available in black and white as well as a range of other colours, it has many uses in general garment sewing. In a foundation garment, wider widths of twill tape are used as bone casings or for reinforcement under a hook and eye closure.

Figure 4.9

Cotton tape

Cotton tape is a strong, non-stretch tape with a plain weave (Figure 4.10). It's available in black and white in a range of widths from 6mm to 25mm (¼"–1") and is used to stabilize and reinforce seams. When building an inner corselette, 6mm (¼") cotton tape can be used to stabilize the neckline, while wider widths can house boning.

Figure 4.10

Seam binding

Seam binding (also called hem binding) is a lightweight, non-stretch ribbon with a satiny sheen and is typically used to finish raw edges on a garment (Figure 4.11). Available in a wide range of colours, it comes in a 1cm (⅜") and a 2.5cm (1") width and may be rayon or a cotton blend. It can be used to bind a raw edge or applied flat to cover the raw edge. For an inner corselette, it may be used to finish the upper and lower edges, to stabilize the neckline or to cover hooks and eyes.

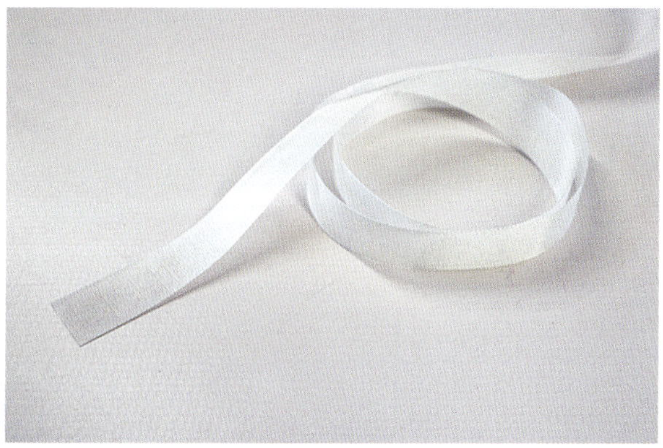

Figure 4.11

Figure 4.12

Bias tape

Bias tape, or bias binding, can be used for facings, for binding seam allowances and for making piping (Figure 4.12). It comes in a range of colours and widths, usually in a cotton or a cotton–polyester blend. You can also make your own from a light to medium-weight fabric. As bias tape has natural stretch, it is suitable for use on curved edges and seams. Its uses in a corselette include binding or facing the upper and lower edges or as a bone casing.

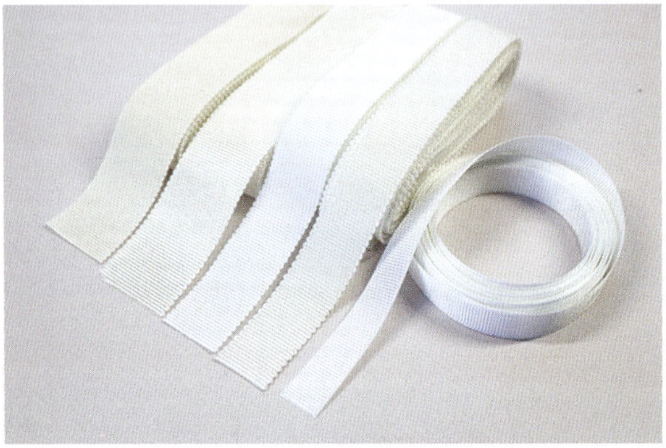

Figure 4.13

Grosgrain and Petersham ribbon

These two ribbons look similar, but they have important differences (Figure 4.13). Grosgrain ribbon is usually made from polyester or nylon and has straight edges. It is a little stiff and cannot be shaped or moulded. Petersham ribbon is made from cotton, rayon or viscose, or a blend of these. It has scalloped edges and can be shaped into a curve with a steam iron. It is strong, but generally softer than grosgrain, and it is the more comfortable of the two for a waist stay. Both ribbons come in a variety of widths, but for an inner corselette, the most commonly used widths range from 1cm to 1.5cm (⅜"–⅝") for boning channels and support for hand-sewn hook and eye closures and 2.5cm (1") for a waist stay.

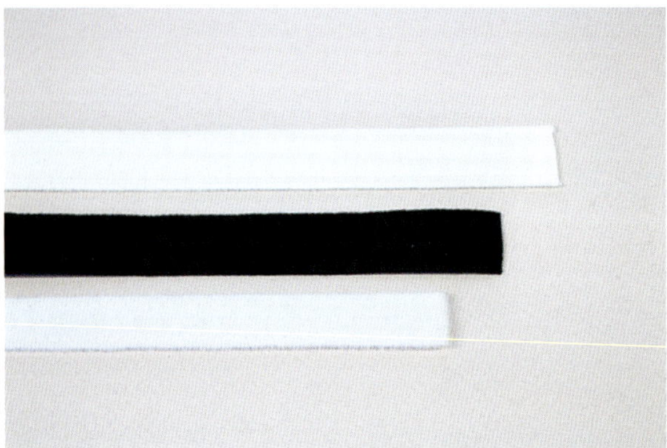

Figure 4.14

Tubular boning tape

Tubular bone casings are flat, hollow fabric tubes with a channel on each side for stitching (Figure 4.14). They fully encase the boning and are ideal for sheer or light-coloured fabrics. They reduce the likelihood of the bones showing on the right side of the garment, although they are a little thicker than other casing materials. They come in black, white and nude and in various sizes to match different boning widths. Tubular casings are available in cotton or a plush backed nylon similar to bra underwire casing.

Fasteners

A corselette fastens with either a zipper or hooks and eyes. Both come in a range of styles and sizes. Selecting the correct one is important to ensure a sturdy, inconspicuous closure.

Zippers

There are many different types of zipper available. A regular dress zipper, a metal zipper or a heavy-duty invisible zipper are the strongest and most suitable for an inner corselette (Figure 4.15). Choose a length that will open to the low hip. Although your corselette will likely finish higher, the zipper needs to open to the widest point of the figure for ease of dressing. Keep in mind, a mesh invisible zipper is generally not considered strong enough to withstand the tension on a corselette.

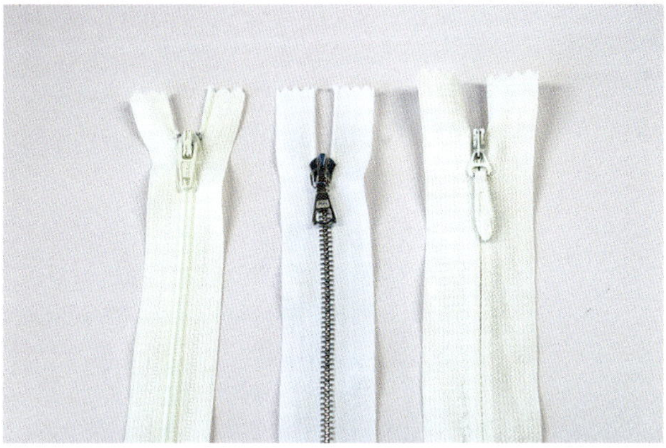

Figure 4.15

Hooks and eyes

There are many types of hook and eye set available – regular, coat, fur and corsetry, as well as wider skirt and trouser fasteners and decorative hook and eye clasps. They range in size from 0 to 3 corresponding to between 6mm and 12mm (¼"–½"). For an inner corselette, choose a smaller-sized (size 1 or 8mm) regular hook and eye set with a round eye (Figure 4.16). As an alternative, a trouser hook and bar can also be used on the waist stay.

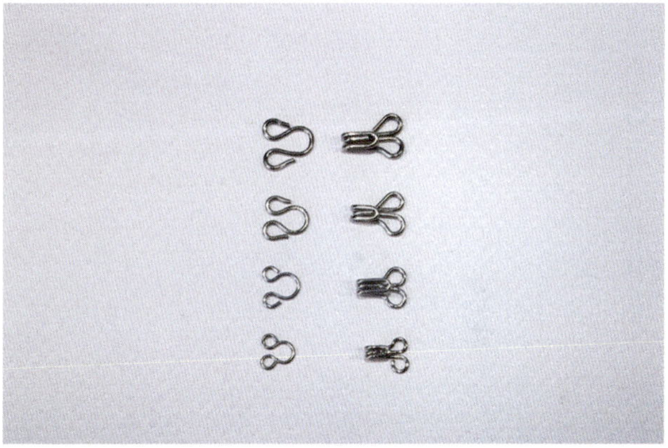

Figure 4.16

Hook and eye tape

Hooks and eyes can be purchased attached to a cotton or nylon tape. There are several styles available; however, an inner corselette uses tape with a single row of hooks and eyes (Figure 4.17). The tape is available in white, black and beige and has a closed width of 2.5cm (1") with the hardware spaced 2cm–2.5cm (¾"–1") apart. The hardware is often centred on a wide tape so that it can enclose a raw edge, but narrower tapes where the hardware is set at the edge can also be found and are less bulky.

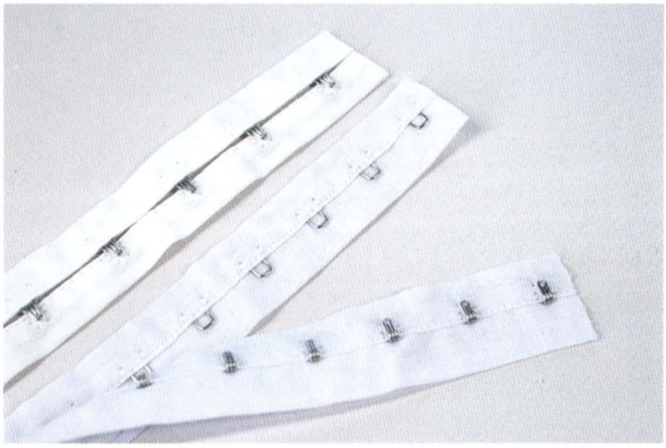

Figure 4.17

5

Construction Overview

The world of inner corselette construction is filled with endless combinations of fabrics, boning, fastenings and techniques to create truly unique garments. Building an inner corselette may appear challenging, but it is not difficult when the construction process is broken into steps. Although the order of some steps can vary, this chapter will provide the framework for building a corselette and joining it to a garment. In the following pages you will learn the steps to build a simple, lightly boned, single-layer corselette. It closes with a zipper and joins to the garment along the upper edge with a facing. This design is the perfect starting point to build experience and confidence before exploring other construction methods.

Prepare the pattern

Check that all changes made during the toile fitting are transferred to the pattern and that seam allowances are added.

- Use a minimum 1.5cm (⅝") seam allowance for princess seams and 2.5cm (1") for the side and centre back (or closure) seams to allow for any adjustments in your final fabric.
- Determine the finishing method at the upper and lower edge of your corselette and add the appropriate allowances to each of them.
- Ensure that all boning placements are marked.

Prepare the fabric elements

Before cutting, pre-treat the fabric to prevent shrinkage after construction. Wash cotton or linen fabrics and press well. Silk fabrics, such as taffeta or organza, should be well steamed. In addition, ensure that all other tapes and ribbons are pre-treated accordingly if they are prone to shrinkage.

General construction sequence

1. Create the shell.
2. Add the bone casings.
3. Finish the lower edge.
4. Add the fastening.
5. Install the boning and stabilize the upper edge.
6. Add the waist stay.
7. Join the corselette to the garment.

Create the shell

1. Cut out the pattern, labelling each piece and transferring pattern markings with waxed tracing paper. Thread trace the upper edge, the placement lines and the opening seamlines (Figure 5.1).

Figure 5.1

2. Sew any darts first and press them to one side, then sew the seams. Clip the seam allowances and press them open over a curved surface (Figure 5.2).

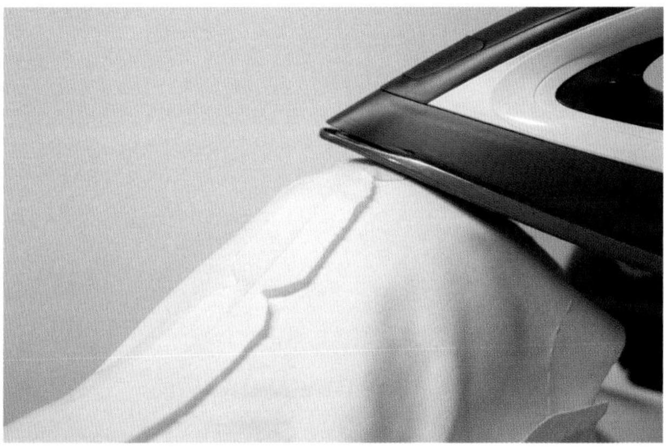

Figure 5.2

3. Finish the seam allowances (Figure 5.3).

Figure 5.3

Add the bone casings

1. Centre the bone casings over the seamlines and pin in place (Figure 5.4).

2. Sew each side of the tape 2mm (⅛") from the edge, sewing from the lower edge to the top. Cut a piece of boning to fit each casing and finish the ends. Slip each piece of boning into its casing to check its fit (adjust the casings if necessary) then set aside until needed (Figure 5.5).

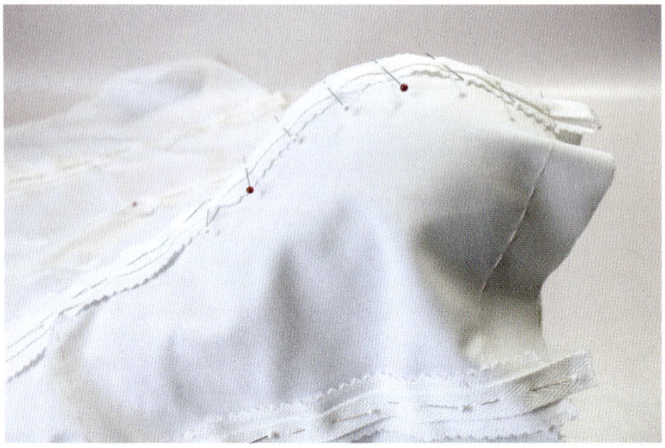

Figure 5.4

Figure 5.5

> **TIP**
>
> When pinning bone casings onto curved areas such as the bust and hips, place the corselette over a curved surface to keep everything smooth.

Finish the lower edge

Sew across the lower seamline and then finish the raw edge (Figure 5.6). In this case, the lower edge has been bound with seam binding.

Figure 5.6

Add the fastening

Insert a zipper in the centre back seam, placing it 2cm (¾") below the neckline (this sets it below the garment closure) (Figure 5.7). Use a centred application and allow the end of the zipper to hang below the lower edge of the corselette.

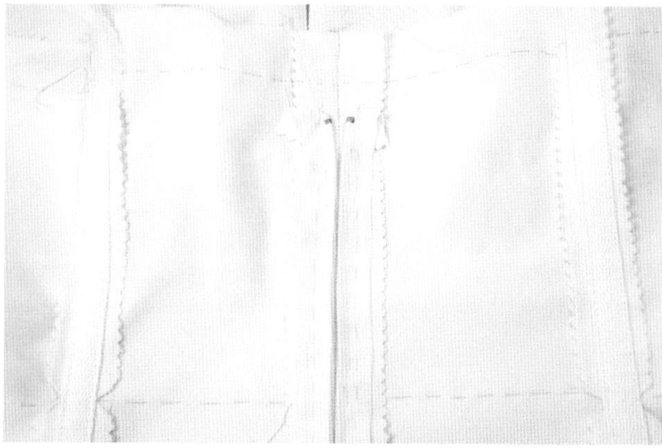

Figure 5.7

Install the boning and stabilize the upper edge

1. Insert the boning into the casings then staystitch across the upper edge, securing the bones (Figure 5.8).

Figure 5.8

2. Baste seam binding over the staystitching to stabilize the upper edge and attach hanging loops at each side seam (Figure 5.9).

Figure 5.9

Add the waist stay

1. Prepare the waist stay. Place it along the waistline with the lower edge resting on the waistline placement line (Figure 5.10).

2. Stitch the stay by hand to each bone casing and also to the corselette 2.5cm (1") from the centre back (Figure 5.11).

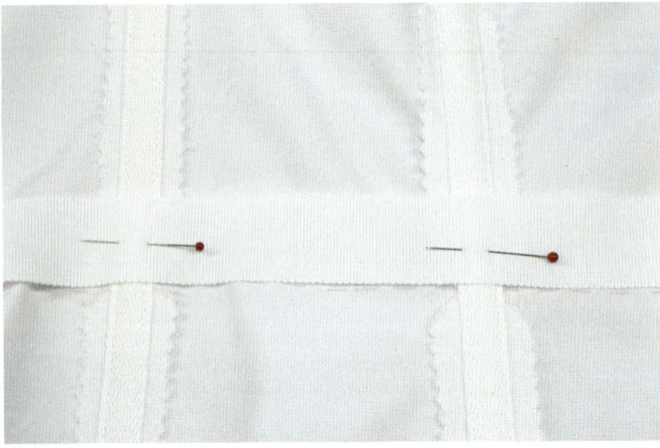

Figure 5.10

Figure 5.11

Join the corselette to the garment

1. Slip the corselette into the completed gown and pin the upper edges together, matching the seamlines (Figure 5.12).

2. Draft a facing from the corselette pattern (see 'Construct a facing', page 99). Cut the facing from the fashion fabric, interface each piece then join them together. Press up the seam allowance on the lower edge (Figure 5.13).

Figure 5.12

Figure 5.13

3. Place the facing over the gown, right sides together. Stitch in place (Figure 5.14).

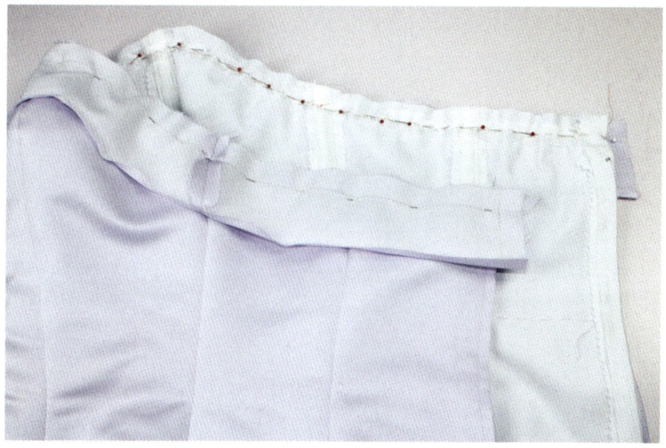

Figure 5.14

4. Understitch the facing. Turn in the ends diagonally and fold the pressed lower edge in place. Slipstitch the facing to the corselette, keeping the outer garment free (Figure 5.15).

Figure 5.15

5. Attach a hook and eye at the top edge of the facing (Figure 5.16).

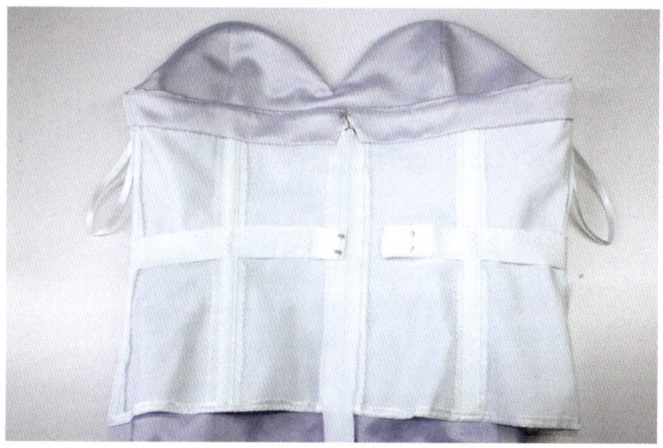

Figure 5.16

6

Creating the Shell

When creating the shell, several things should be taken into consideration to choose the best construction technique for each project. What type of fabric are you using? How much support does the garment need and how much wear will it receive? Additionally, you will want to consider how the corselette and the garment will be joined, what you want the finished product to look like and whether it may need alterations in the future. Three methods are commonly used to construct the shell: single layer, double layer and lined. While each has a different finish, all methods follow a similar process and will give good results.

Single, double or lined?

So, which method is the best for your project?

Single-layer corselette

A single-layer corselette can be used if less support is required, or where a firmer fabric is used such as drill or coutil. The seam allowances need to be finished, as they are visible, but this style of corselette is easy to fit and alter.

Double-layer corselette

A double-layer corselette has each pair of panels joined at the beginning of construction and then treated as one. With the seams and bone casings remaining visible, it is easier to alter, but the seam allowances need to be finished. Most light to medium-weight fabrics are suitable for a double-layer construction, and it is the best method for mesh fabrics such as bobbinet.

Lined corselette

A lined corselette is constructed as two separate layers (a main and a lining) which are joined wrong sides together. This creates a clean finish on the inside, hiding any construction elements. It does make the corselette more difficult to alter, though, so be sure to perfect the fit with a toile.

Assembling a single-layer corselette is discussed in Chapter 5, so let's look at the different ways to build a corselette shell with two layers.

TIP

When two layers are being used in a corselette, they can be cut on the same grain or, for added strength, on opposite grains. For ease, to use opposite grains, mark both grainlines on your pattern pieces (Figure 6.1).

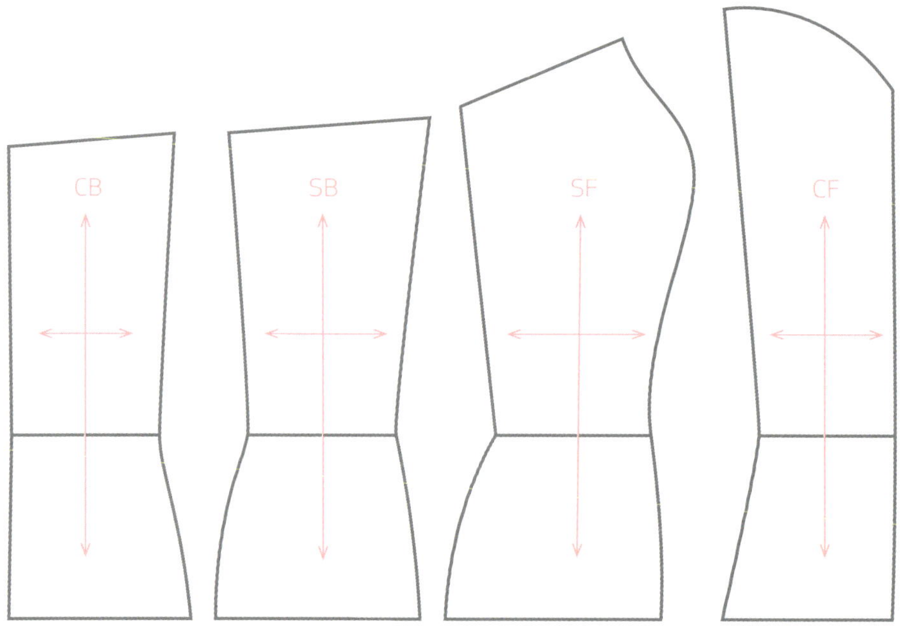

Figure 6.1

Assembling a lined corselette

1. Prepare the pattern pieces, marking the seamlines and bone placements, as well as the grainlines you intend to use. Cut one set of panels (the main layer) (Figure 6.2).

2. Using waxed tracing paper, transfer the pattern markings and bone placement lines to the fabric and label each piece (Figure 6.3).

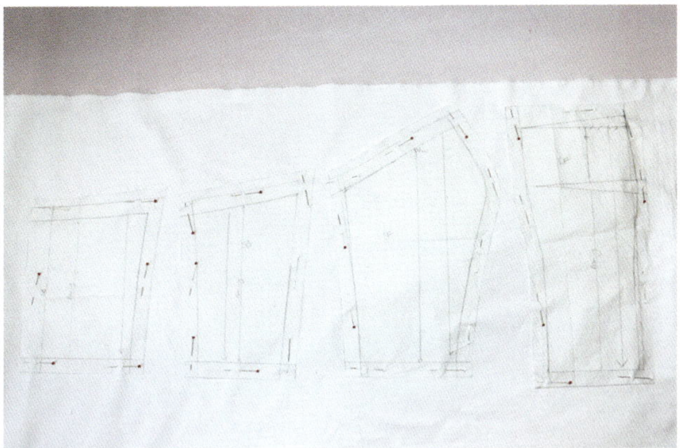

Figure 6.2

Figure 6.3

3. Stitch and press the darts then the seams. Trim and clip the seam allowances and press them open. This layer will be used to house the boning and fastening (Figure 6.4).

4. Cut a second set of panels for the lining using the opposite grain if you wish. Mark the seamlines (bone placement isn't necessary) and label each piece. Repeat Step 2 to construct the lining, setting it aside until needed (Figure 6.5).

Figure 6.4

Figure 6.5

Assembling a double-layer woven corselette

1. Cut your first set of panels. Using waxed tracing paper and a tracing wheel, transfer the pattern markings to both layers, including the grainline you want to use for the second layer (Figure 6.6).

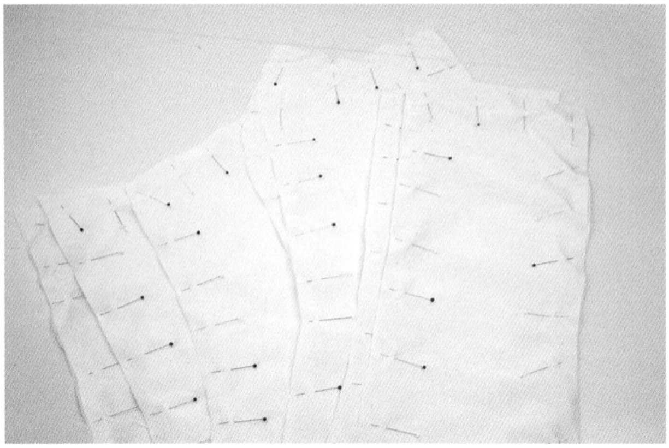

Figure 6.6

2. Separate the panels and lay them out on a single layer of fabric (using the opposite grain if you wish). Pin through all layers then cut the second set of panels (Figure 6.7).

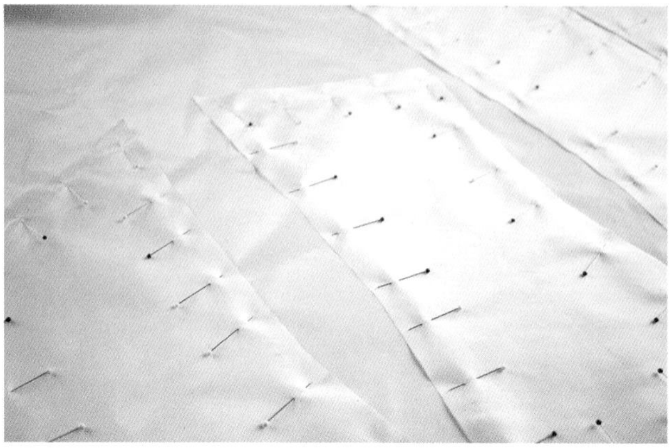

Figure 6.7

3. Keeping the two fabric layers pinned together, thread trace the stitching lines for the darts and seams, securing both layers together (Figure 6.8).

Figure 6.8

4. Stitch and press the darts then the seams. Trim and clip the seam allowances, press them open then finish the raw edges (Figure 6.9).

Figure 6.9

Assembling a double-layer bobbinet corselette

1. Create a full set of pattern pieces and mark each with the lengthwise and crosswise grain. Remove the seam allowances and carefully cut away the dart volume (Figure 6.10).

2. Lay out the paper pattern in a single layer on the lengthwise grain. Cut out, leaving at least 2.5cm (1") seam allowances around each pattern piece. Keeping the pattern pinned to the fabric, lay the pieces on the crosswise grain and pin in place through all layers. Cut the second fabric layer (Figure 6.11).

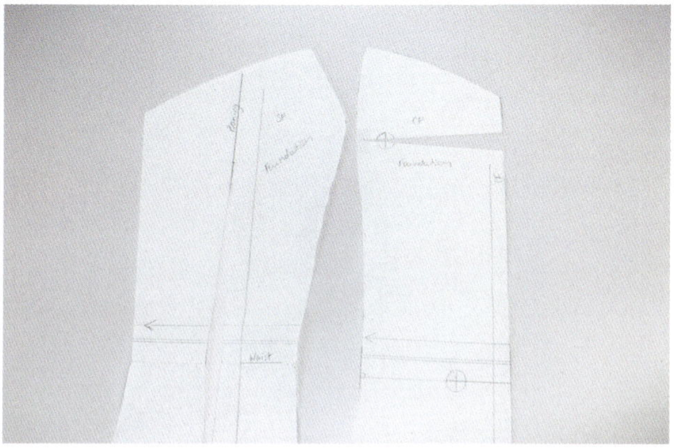

Figure 6.10

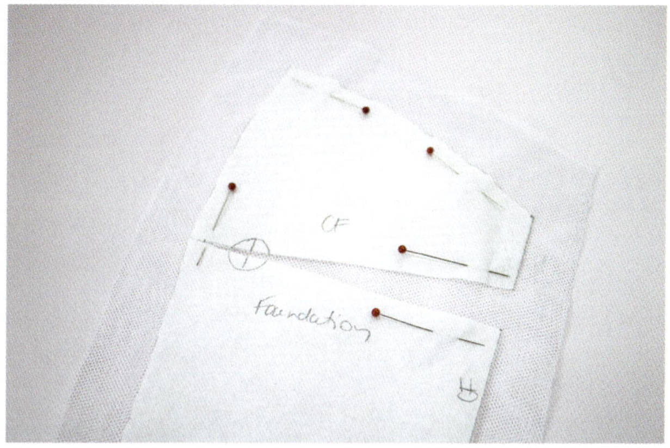

Figure 6.11

3. Before removing the paper pattern, use it as a guide to thread trace the seams and darts and any other pertinent information, for example boning placement, the waistline and seamlines for matching with the outer garment (Figure 6.12).

4. Stitch and press the darts then sew the seams. Trim and clip the seam allowances, press them open and finish the raw edges (Figure 6.13).

Figure 6.12

Figure 6.13

Construction basics

The final outcome of a custom corselette depends heavily on the quality of the construction. Investing the time and effort in this step is critical to ensure that your project not only turns out looking neat and professional but is also comfortable and robust. Seams should be smooth and free of puckers, while being strong enough to hold up under tension. Visible seam allowances should be treated to prevent fraying, ensuring their durability. Take the time to test your stitch quality and make samples of seam treatments before you begin. These steps will result in a successful garment that you will wear with confidence.

Pressing

Good pressing is essential for achieving a professional finish and should occur throughout construction. It's also important to press all fabrics and pattern pieces before beginning. Any creases in these distorts the grainline during the layout. Begin by pressing a scrap to determine the best approach for your fabric. Check the correct iron temperature and whether steam will mark the fabric. Be careful not to over-press as the impression of seam allowances and their finishes can be left on the right side. Use a press cloth if you feel that the fabric should be protected.

Figure 6.14

To get professional results there are many excellent pressing aids available (Figure 6.14). A tailor's ham and sleeve roll, as well as a pressing cloth are among the most useful aids. While not essential, a pressing mould for bra cups is also very helpful in shaping and pressing the bust area.

After stitching, press each seam or dart flat as sewn to set the stitches. Next, press the seam open from the wrong side, then press again from the right side, using a pressing cloth if necessary. Always press curved seams and areas over a curved surface to build shape into your corselette. Darts should be pressed before they are sewn into a seam, and all seams should be pressed before they are crossed with another seam.

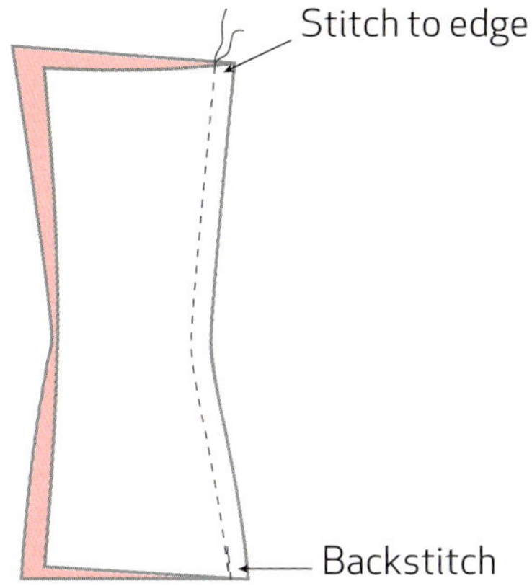

Figure 6.15

Sewing the seams

Corselettes require a seam that will hold up under the tension placed on it by the wearer. Of course, using a high-quality thread is important, but testing your thread, stitch length and machine tension before sewing the seams is equally essential. This is done by creating a sample composed of the same layers as the corselette. When assessing the seam strength, it's important to consider the unique properties of the fabric, how snug the corselette fit is and the amount of wear it will receive. If there is strain on the seams, consider strengthening them by sewing a second row of stitches on top of the first using a different stitch length. Stitching bone casings over the seams will also provide added strength.

When sewing the seams, use a medium-length straight stitch. At the lower edge, it is best to backstitch, particularly if the edge will be finished by hand (Figure 6.15). To prevent puckering, sew all seams in the same direction: from the lower edge to the upper edge. Press the seam after it is sewn and then trim and notch the seam allowances. Finish the edges if necessary. Pressing the seams open will give a flatter finish, although some curvier seams, such as those over the bust, may sit more smoothly when pressed to one side. Seams should be pressed and the edges finished before they are crossed by another seam.

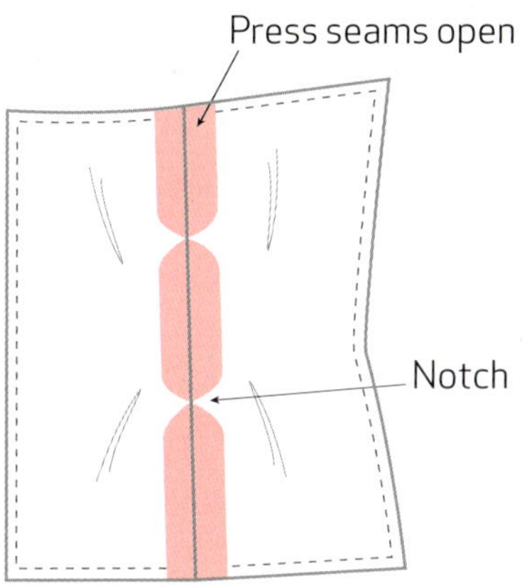

Figure 6.16

Notching the seam allowances

Due to the curved nature of seams in a corselette, the seam allowances will need to be notched, enabling them to lie flat. On a curved seam, the stitching line is a different length than the cut edge and if the allowances aren't notched, they will pull or bunch when pressed open. Many couture and historical garments use curved notches, making it easier to apply the traditional seam finishes of binding or hand overcasting, but a triangular notch works fine too. Notch only where needed, keeping the inner point about 6mm (¼") away from the seamline. Begin by notching each seam at the waistline then notch the front princess seams at the bust point and the underbust point. Make further notches as necessary so that the seams lay flat, remembering that curvy figures are likely to need more notches than straight figures (Figure 6.16).

Finishing the seam allowances

If the seam allowances will be visible on the inside of the corselette, the cut edges will need to be finished. This prevents fraying, as well as serving to hold the two layers together in a double-layer corselette. Seam finishes should be soft and comfortable while adding little bulk. Hand overcasting is my favourite method as it gives a lovely finish and doesn't add stiffness to the fabric. However, it is more time-consuming and there are quicker alternatives. Choose one of the following to finish the raw edges.

Hand overcast

Using a single thread and a small needle, make small slanted stitches over the raw edge. Keep the stitches shallow and about 3mm–5mm (⅛"–¼") apart (Figure 6.17).

Figure 6.17

Pinked

Pinking is best suited to a single layer of fabric. Use pinking shears to trim the seam allowances to 1.5cm–2cm (⅝"–¾"). If desired, first sew a row of straight stitching 6mm (¼") from the raw edge (Figure 6.18).

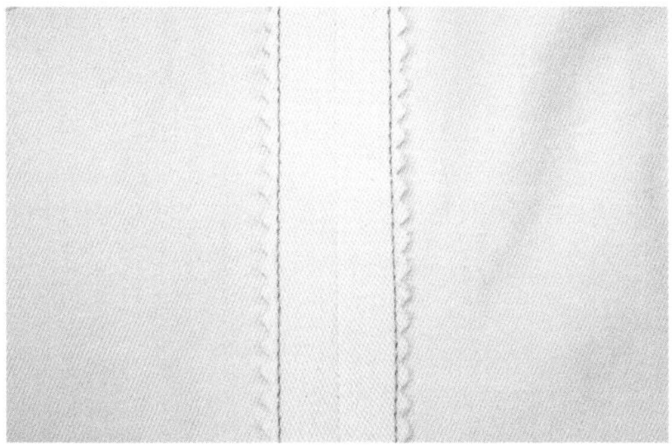

Figure 6.18

Zigzag

Use a medium zigzag and stitch near the cut edge then trim the seam allowance close to the stitching (Figure 6.19).

Figure 6.19

Overlock stitch

This finish creates the most bulk over the raw edge. Use a 3-thread stitch as this encases the edge with less thread than a 4-thread stitch (Figure 6.20).

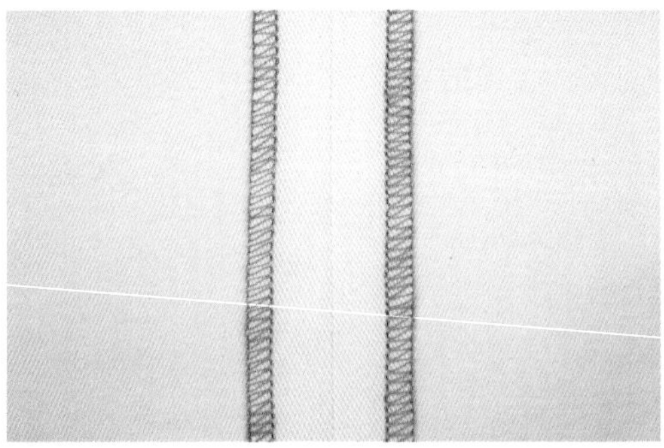

Figure 6.20

7

Installing the Boning

Boning is really the key element that helps a corselette maintain its desired shape and perform its role. It adds structure and stretches the fabric to create a sturdy base to both smooth the figure and support the outer garment. Regardless of which type of boning you choose, taking the time to plan the boning layout and deciding the best method to install your boning will result in a corselette that offers the right level of support. Of course, experimenting with the layout during the toile fitting will give a good indication of where boning is required. Be prepared to refine the placement in the fashion fabric if necessary.

LIGHT TO MEDIUM SUPPORT

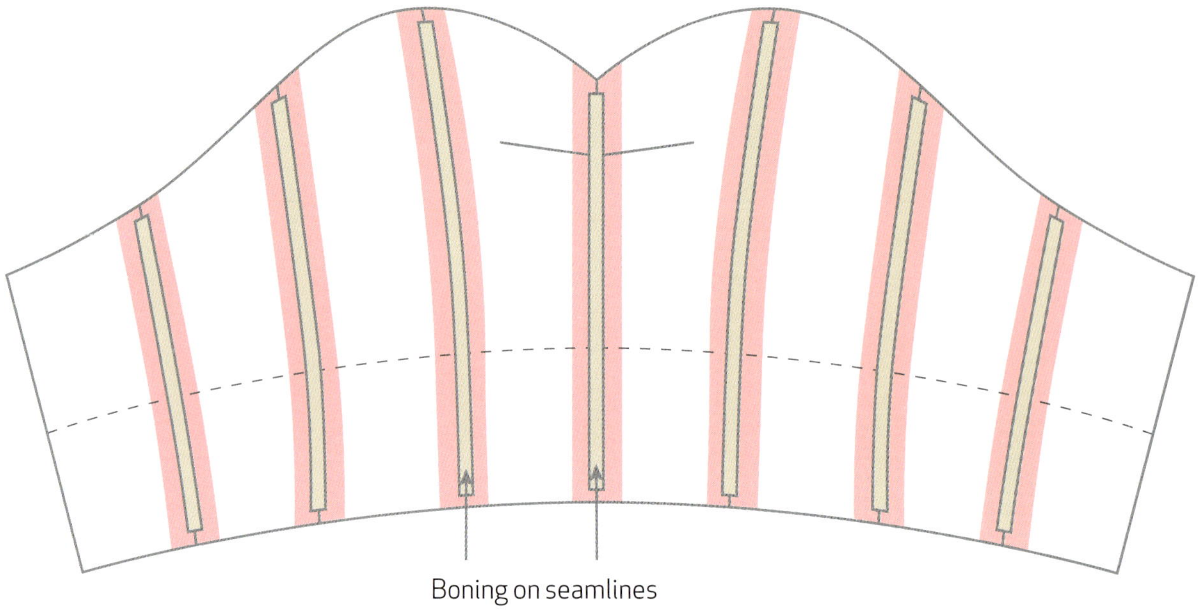

Figure 7.1

MEDIUM TO FIRM SUPPORT

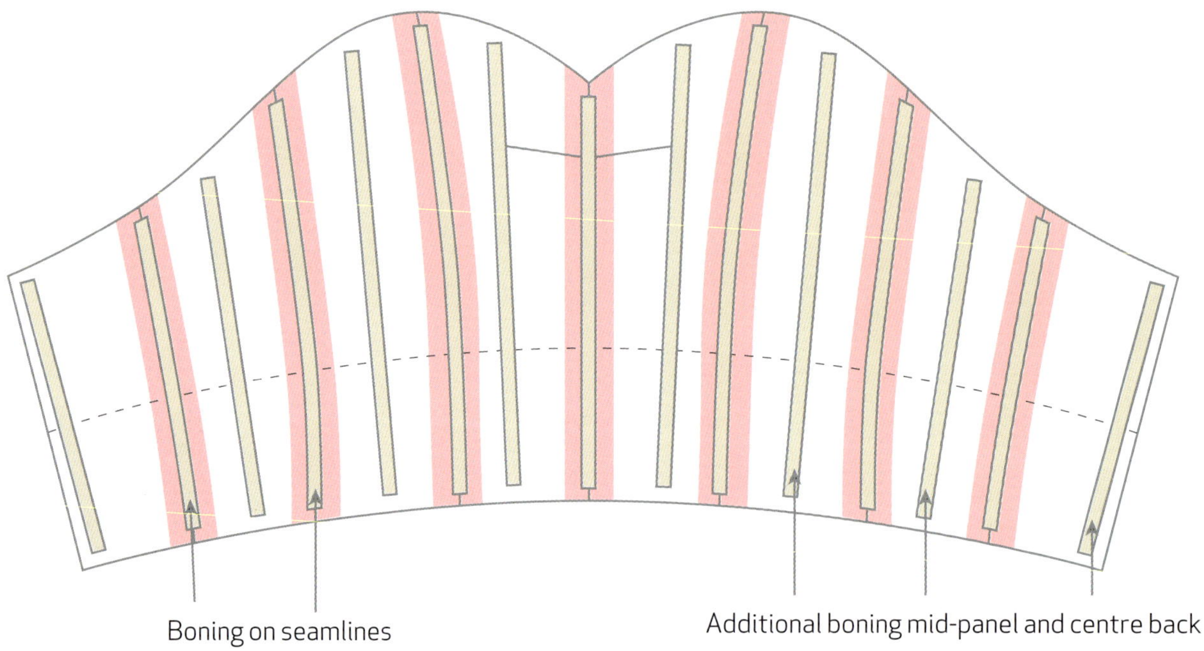

Figure 7.2

Boning layout

Both the amount of boning needed and the placement of the boning depends on the size and shape of the wearer's figure as well as the design of the outer garment. Because of this there is no 'correct' layout – boning should be placed wherever it's required to achieve its purpose. It can be placed on the seamlines, in the centre of panels, over vertical darts, or any combination of these. Bones can be applied in single pieces or side by side in pairs for added strength. Applying the boning on seamlines, or in a tubular casing in the middle of a panel, provides a buffer to help the boning remain hidden when viewed from the outside of the garment.

The best place to start when figuring out how much boning to use and where to place it is with your toile. Start by placing bones on each seamline then use the fitting to determine where extra boning is needed (Figure 7.1). Larger figures or fuller busts will benefit from having more bones, as will a bodice supporting a heavy skirt or weighty embellishments (Figure 7.2). Check that the type and the position of the bones provide sufficient support and comfort for the wearer. As a guide, aim to place one bone every 7.5cm–10cm (3"–4") at the waist level. If areas of the garment are sagging and crumpling during the fitting, add extra bones in those areas.

Preparing the boning

Boning is generally purchased in continuous lengths and cut to size. One exception is spiral steel boning, which can be purchased in pre-finished lengths. These are simpler to use, but a continuous roll is more economical. You can cut and finish the correct lengths as needed. To determine the required length for each bone, measure the length of the bone placement lines, excluding seam allowances, then subtract 6mm (¼"). Bones should be about 6mm (¼") shorter than the seam length and no less than 3mm (⅛") shorter, so that they don't exert tension along the edges. Cut bones to match each of your measurements and finish the ends (see 'Boning', pages 34–8, for finishing the ends of boning).

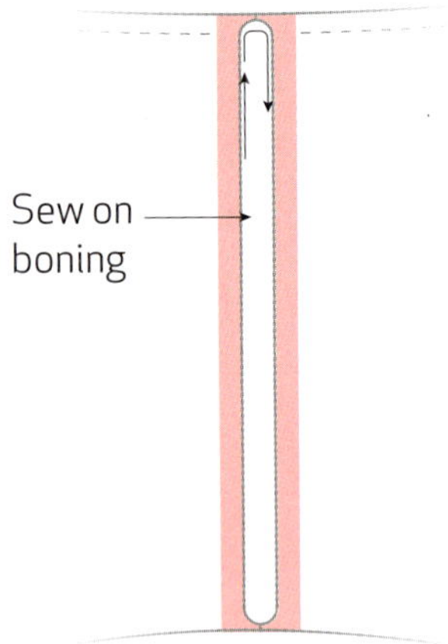

Figure 7.3

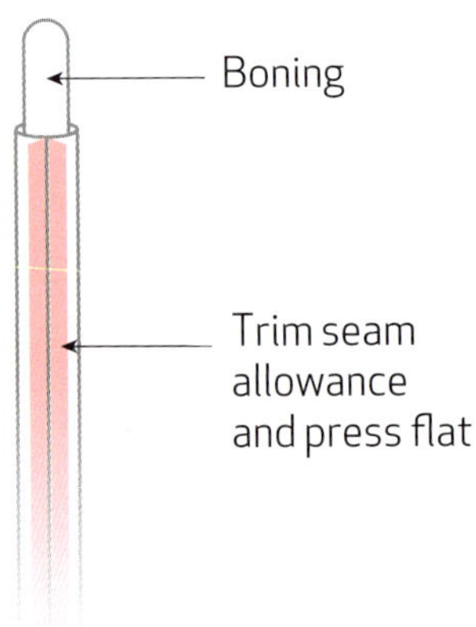

Figure 7.4

Installing the boning

The way you install your boning will depend on the type of boning chosen and the construction method used for your corselette. Two types of plastic bones (woven polyester boning and reinforced plastic boning) can be sewn through if desired, but all other bones require a casing or channel.

Sewn to the fabric

Both woven polyester boning and reinforced (German) plastic bones can be stitched directly onto the fabric, either mid panel or centred over the seams and darts. Cut the bones to the correct length and finish the ends. Sew down both lengthwise edges and across the ends to secure the bone to the fabric (Figure 7.3).

Casings

Boning is usually housed in a casing that can be attached in one of two ways: extended to the edges of the garment, or turned under one or both ends of the bone. While extending the casing from edge to edge gives uniform support along the placement line, it does create extra bulk at the upper and lower edges. Depending on the design of the garment and its edge finish, this may not be desirable. To reduce bulk in the upper or lower seamline, or when the bone is shorter than the full length of the seam, the end of the casing can be turned under, creating a pocket in which to slip the bone. It's best to make a sample using your combination of casing, corselette layers and edge finishes to see which method will give the best result.

When attaching the casing, the space between the two rows of stitching should be around 3mm (⅛") wider than the bone. If the space is too wide, the bone won't be snug enough and will stand on its side. To ensure that the correct-sized spacing is used, sample the distance between your two rows of stitching before beginning.

There are several suitable options for bone casings. Cotton or twill tape, Petersham ribbon, bias tape and tubular bone casings have been discussed previously (see 'Tapes', pages 39–40). Another option is to create your own casings from strips of a lightweight, densely woven fabric. The corselette fabric is often ideal. Cut strips of fabric on the bias or straight grain to fit the width of the bone, plus a seam allowance. Stitch the fabric into a tube then press the seam open and position it centrally on the underside (Figure 7.4).

Sewing on a casing

1. Cut lengths of the casing to match each placement line between the edges of the corselette.
2. Centre the casing over the seamline or placement mark and stitch down each long edge, stitching both sides in the same direction to prevent the fabric twisting (Figure 7.5).
3. Slip the bone into the casing to check the fit.

To finish the casing at bust level, mark the placement line for the bone on the centre front seamline. Cut the casing, allowing a 1cm (⅜") turn-in at the upper end. Centre the casing over the seamline, placing the folded edge over the placement line. Stitch along both sides of the casing and across the upper edge (Figure 7.6). Slip the bone into the casing from the lower edge to check its fit.

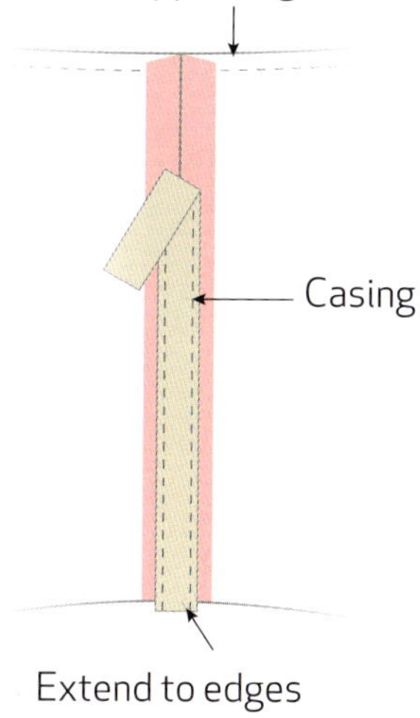

Figure 7.5

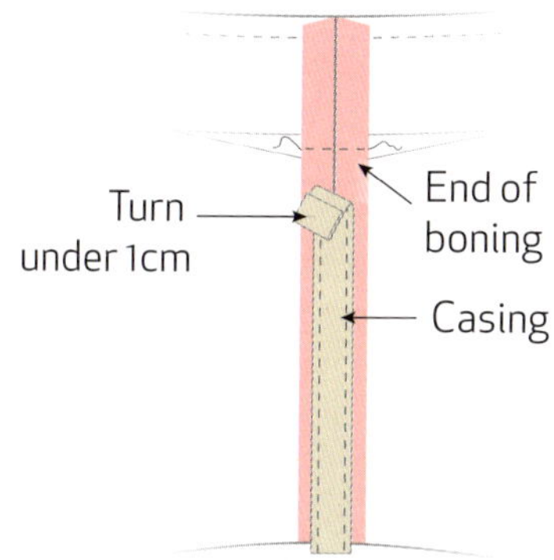

Figure 7.6

Channels

In a lined corselette, boning can be inserted into a channel sewn between the two layers. This gives a clean finish on the inside and eliminates any unnecessary bulk from sewn-on casings. Accuracy is key when joining the two corselette shells before creating the channels.

Sewing a channel

1. Sew both layers of the shell as for a lined corselette (see 'Assembling a lined corselette', page 53).
2. Place the layers wrong sides together, carefully matching seamlines and the upper and lower edges. If preferred, baste the seamlines together to hold them securely.
3. Make double rows of stitching through both layers on the seamlines and the mid panel where desired, to fit the width of your boning (Figure 7.7).

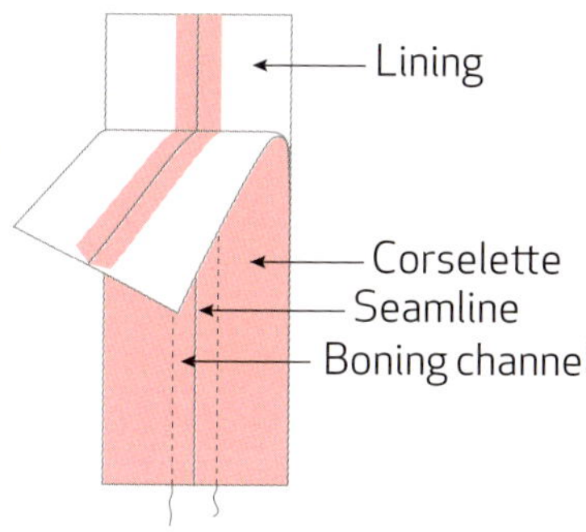

Figure 7.7

8

Edge Finishes

A range of upper and lower edge finishes can be used in corselette construction. They secure the boning and ensure that the corselette's edges stay firm and durable throughout its use. Areas prone to stretching and distortion from wear need to first be reinforced and stabilized. The edges are then finished to protect them and prevent fraying. To choose the best methods for each project, consider the shape of the upper edge and how much reinforcement is needed, as well as how the corselette and the garment will be joined. Also consider the fabric and construction method used. As always, making some samples will establish which methods are the most suitable for each project.

Stabilizing the upper edge

The upper edge of most strapless designs is at minimum slightly off grain. Stabilizing this edge helps prevent stretching and gaping during wear. In addition, it gives the opportunity to cup the front edge over the bust and allows the boning to be held close to the body. This is particularly important in designs with sweetheart and V-shaped upper edges. Unless the upper edge is fairly straight, it is likely to gape around the curves of the bust. Easing the front panels onto a tape will help solve this issue. The shape of the neckline and the cup size will determine the amount of ease possible and can be determined during a fitting. The seamline should first be stabilized with staystitching before adding a tape to further strengthen and shape the edge. Seam binding, strips of silk organza, and cotton tape are all suitable choices for this purpose. Using a lightweight tape such as seam binding or silk organza is best when the corselette and the garment will be joined at the upper edge by machine, to reduce bulk in the seamline. Any of the tapes mentioned can be used to stabilize and shape the upper edge when the corselette will be joined to the garment by hand.

Adding a lightweight stay

Staystitch the upper edge of the corselette on the seamline. Beginning at the centre back (or opening edge), centre the tape over the seamline (Figure 8.1). Keep the tape the same length as the seamline across the back, then build between 1cm and 1.5cm (⅜"–⅝") of ease into the corselette in each half of the front. For straight upper edges, a small amount of easing over the side front panel should be sufficient. For corselettes with a sweetheart or V-shaped upper edge, add additional easing over the centre front panel (Figure 8.2). Baste the stay in place.

Figure 8.1

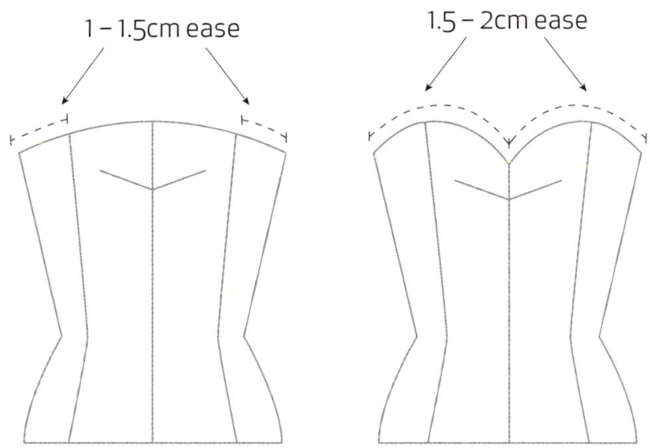

Figure 8.2

Adding a cotton tape stay

As cotton tape is a little thicker, it's best placed on the seam allowance, just next to the staystitching, rather than centred over the seamline. Staystitch the upper edge of the corselette on the seamline. Place the tape on the seam allowance, just above the staystitching (Figure 8.3). Apply it in the same manner as for a lightweight stay: in a 1:1 ratio across the back and then easing the upper edge onto the tape slightly, as needed, over the front panels. Stitch the tape in place along the lower edge with a small running stitch.

Figure 8.3

Upper edge finishes

Once stabilized, the upper edge of the corselette is ready to be joined to the garment using a machine method. However, when joining the corselette to the garment by hand, it is necessary to first finish the upper edge of the corselette. The finishes range from functional to decorative and should be chosen according to the method by which the corselette will join to the garment.

Hemmed edge

A narrow hem is a versatile finish and can be applied to most upper edge designs. In its simplest form it can be used for the wrapped edge joining method, where it is hidden underneath the garment facing (Figure 8.4). If the edge of the corselette will be visible, the hemmed edge can be bound or covered with tape.

Figure 8.4

1. When preparing the pattern, allow a 1cm–1.5cm-wide (⅜"–⅝"-wide) hem allowance on the upper edge.
2. Reinforce the upper edge with staystitching and tape.
3. Turn the hem allowance to the inside and catch-stitch it to the corselette.

Bound edge

This finish is ideal if the upper edge of the corselette may be glimpsed during wear, such as when it is not connected to the garment at the upper edge. The bound edge method uses a bias strip, usually of the fashion fabric, to enclose the upper edge of the corselette (Figure 8.5). The edge is first finished with a narrow hem and then the binding is applied. Mark a narrow 1cm–1.5cm (⅜"–⅝") hem allowance above the upper edge of the pattern.

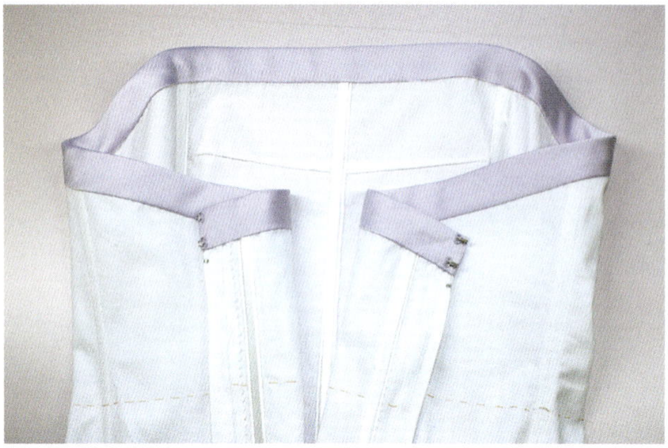

Figure 8.5

1. Staystitch the upper edge and add stay tape.
2. Turn the hem allowance to the inside and stitch to the corselette by hand.
3. Determine the width of your finished binding, usually 3.5cm–4cm (1⅜"–1⅝"), and cut a strip of the fashion fabric that is double this width, plus hem turnings.
4. Fold the bias strip in half lengthwise and turn in the long edges. Place the binding fold along the top edge of the corselette, turning in the ends at the opening edge. Slipstitch the binding in place around all edges. If the upper edge is angled at the centre front, mitre the binding to conform to the shape.

Bias or tape facing

This method is a good choice when joining with the tiered edges method as the upper edge of the corselette will be visible inside the garment. Applying a bias tape or narrow ribbon will create a sturdy yet neat finish (Figure 8.6). When the upper edge of the corselette is straight then a straight-edged tape or ribbon is suitable, but if the edge is curved, use bias tape or Petersham ribbon shaped to fit the design.

Figure 8.6

1. Begin by following Steps 1 and 2 for a 'Hemmed edge'.
2. Cut a length of tape or ribbon to fit the upper edge, if necessary shaping it with steam to match the upper edge shape.
3. Position the tape so that it covers the raw edge of the hem allowance and stitch the upper edge to the corselette by hand or machine.
4. Fold the hem allowance down and sew the lower edge to the corselette.

Clean finish

In a lined corselette, the two layers can be seamed together along the upper edge for a clean finish (Figure 8.7). This method can be applied to any upper edge shape and is suitable for any of the joining methods, although it is best suited to the tiered edges method.

1. To prepare the pattern, add a 1.5cm (⅝") seamline at the upper edge.
2. Construct the shell then stabilize the upper edge of one layer with tape.
3. Place the two layers right sides together and stitch along the upper edge. Trim and clip the seam allowances, then press them towards the lining and understitch them.
4. Turn the lining to the inside and complete the corselette by adding the fastening and finishing the lower edge as applicable for your design.

Figure 8.7

Extended facing

Couture designs often use extended facings as it eliminates a seam at the edge, giving a softer, rounded finish (Figure 8.8). The facing is usually 2.5cm–3cm (1"–1¼") wide and is best used if the upper edge is straight or gently curved. This finish is best for the 'floating edge' joining method or when the corselette has an overlay of fashion fabric.

1. When preparing the pattern, mark the upper edge as a foldline and add the desired facing depth on each panel. Turn the pattern down along the foldline and true the pattern at each seam.
2. Assemble the corselette then staystitch the upper edge just outside the foldline.
3. On the inside, attach tape along the foldline for extra stability. Centre a lightweight tape over the foldline, or if using a sturdier tape, place it on the facing next to the foldline.
4. Neaten the raw edge of the facing with narrow tape or hand overcasting, or by turning it under.
5. Fold the facing inside along the foldline and secure to the corselette by hand.

Figure 8.8

Finishing the lower edge

The lower edge of a corselette is generally given the minimal treatment required to prevent it from unravelling. The goal is to make the edge as invisible as possible under the garment. For zipper closures, the lower edge is finished before the zipper is installed. For hook and eye closures, the order is reversed; the fastenings are attached first then the lower edge is finished.

For a simple yet functional finish, choose one of the options given for finishing the seam allowances: hand overcasting, zigzag stitch, pinking or overlocking (see 'Finishing the seam allowances', page 58). Alternatively, you could use one of the following, more robust finishes.

Hem lace

When applying this finish, the boning ends at a stitching line 6mm (¼") above the lower edge (Figure 8.9). Insert the boning then staystitch along the stitching line. Finish the lower edge with one of the seam finishing methods to prevent unravelling. Next, pin the lace scallop-side down along the stitching line, turning in the ends at the opening edges. Stitch by hand or machine (Figure 8.10).

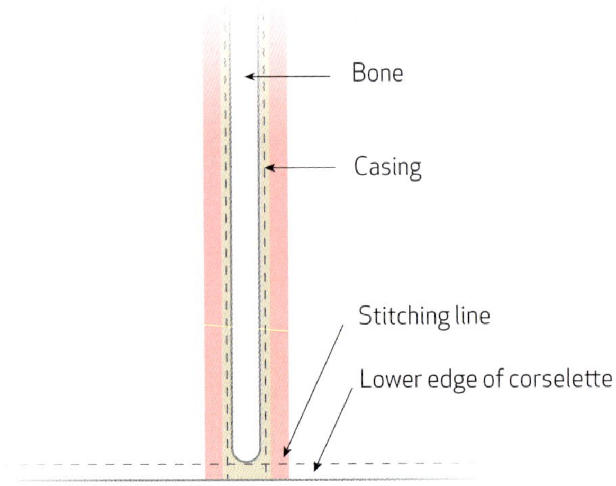

Figure 8.9

Figure 8.10

Clean finished

This finish can be used when the corselette has a main and a lining layer. When cutting, include a seam allowance along the lower edge. Construct the two layers then place them right sides together and stitch along the hemline. Trim the seam allowances and understitch the lining. Turn the lining to the inside and press the lower edge (Figure 8.11).

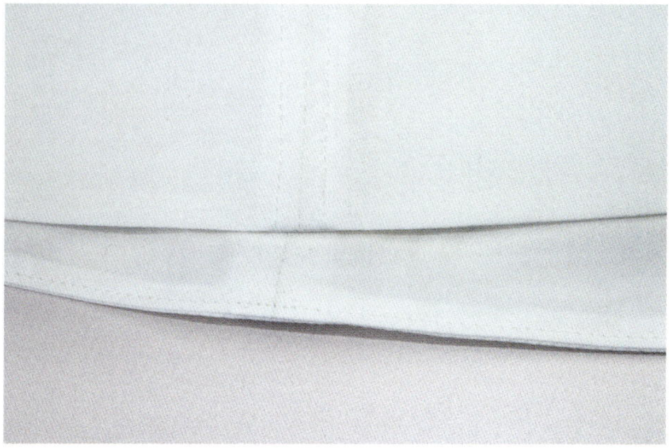

Figure 8.11

Petersham ribbon

In a waist-length corselette, the lower edge can be finished with a length of Petersham ribbon (Figure 8.12). This finishes the edge while also providing the stability needed at the waistline. Attach the lower edge of the ribbon to the corselette by machine. Finish securing it by stitching along the upper edge through all layers, avoiding the boning channels. Alternatively, from the right side stitch through all layers at each seamline, sewing exactly on the stitching line for the bone casing (Figure 8.13).

Figure 8.12

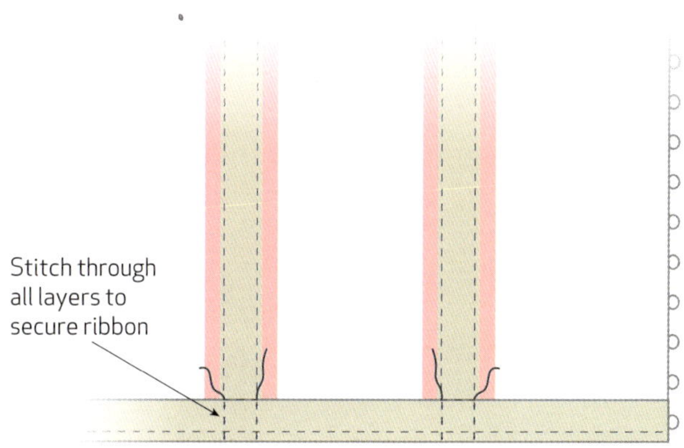

Figure 8.13

Binding

A bound lower edge is a suitable finish for all styles of corselette. Seam binding or bias tape is a good choice for finishing corselettes of heavier-weight fabrics (Figure 8.14). Self-fabric is often used for corselettes constructed from lighter-weight or mesh fabrics (Figure 8.15). When preparing the pattern, mark a stitching line 6mm (¼") above the lower edge and finish the boning here (see Figure 8.9). Staystitch across the stitching line to secure the boning, then bind the allowance.

Figure 8.14

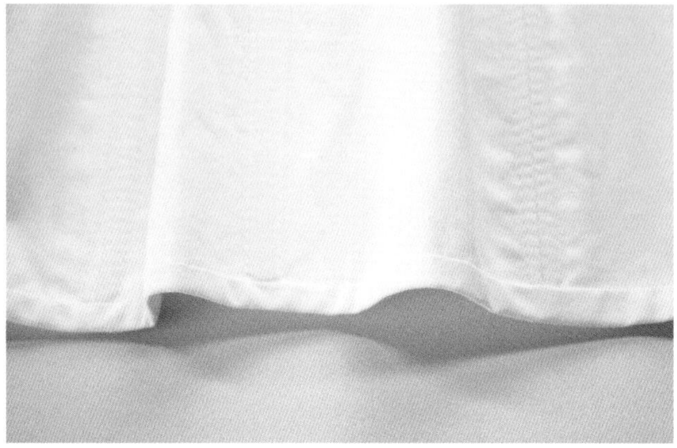

Figure 8.15

9

Adding the Fastening

An inner corselette must have a fastening that's strong and comfortable, yet unobtrusive. When planning the closure, consider the overall design of the corselette. How is it joined to the outer garment? How will the wearer access the fastening? Closures are commonly located at the centre back, but can also be found on the side or centre front. The corselette and the outer garment frequently have separate closures, sometimes with different fastening mechanisms; however, when the fit of the corselette and the outer garment is the same through the bodice, they can be joined and use one closure. In more complex designs, the inner corselette and the garment may have their closures located in different places.

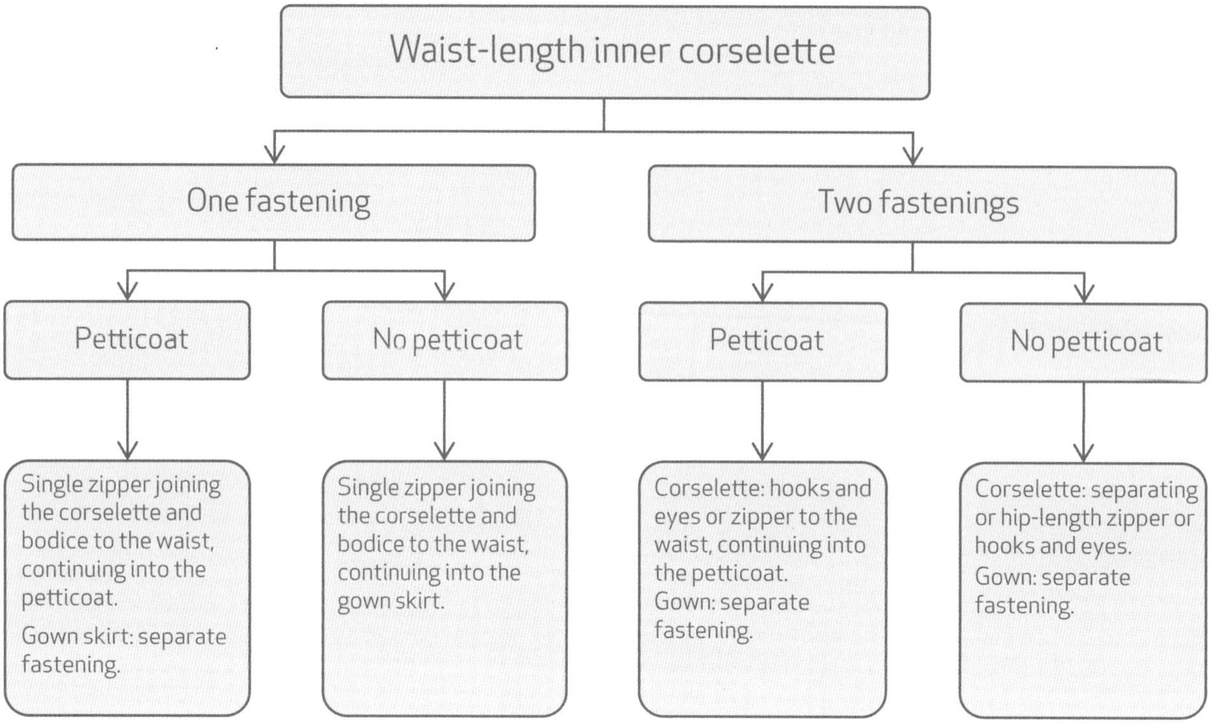

Waist-length inner corselette
One fastening
Two fastenings
Petticoat
No petticoat
Petticoat
No petticoat
Single zipper joining the corselette and bodice to the waist, continuing into the petticoat.
Gown skirt: separate fastening.
Single zipper joining the corselette and bodice to the waist, continuing into the gown skirt.
Corselette: hooks and eyes or zipper to the waist, continuing into the petticoat.
Gown: separate fastening.
Corselette: separating or hip-length zipper or hooks and eyes.
Gown: separate fastening.

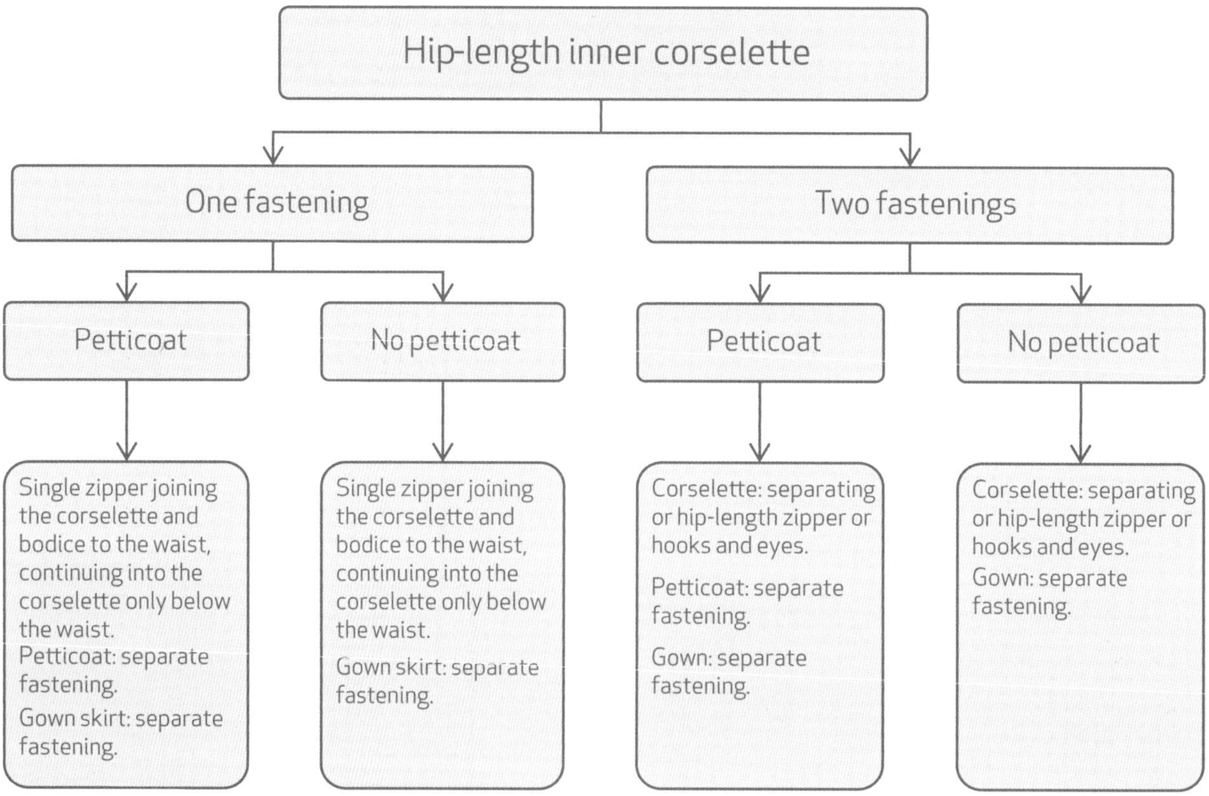

Hip-length inner corselette
One fastening
Two fastenings
Petticoat
No petticoat
Petticoat
No petticoat
Single zipper joining the corselette and bodice to the waist, continuing into the corselette only below the waist.
Petticoat: separate fastening.
Gown skirt: separate fastening.
Single zipper joining the corselette and bodice to the waist, continuing into the corselette only below the waist.
Gown skirt: separate fastening.
Corselette: separating or hip-length zipper or hooks and eyes.
Petticoat: separate fastening.
Gown: separate fastening.
Corselette: separating or hip-length zipper or hooks and eyes.
Gown: separate fastening.

Planning the fastenings

A corselette is part of at least one other garment and often several other garments. These can include the outer bodice, a skirt and petticoats. It is difficult to discuss the fastening of the corselette without considering the other closures required as they are integral to the decision-making process. Because of this, it's best to describe the entire design as a system. The two flow charts shown here will help you select a suitable fastening for your project.

First, decide the length of your corselette as there are subtle differences in the way their fastenings are handled, particularly in joining skirts and petticoats.

Next, assess the fit of the garment bodice to determine if you'll use one or two fastenings. Traditionally the corselette has a separate fastening from the outer garment. This method works with any design and is essential if the outer garment has more ease than the corselette above the waistline. If the garment has the same circumference as the corselette above the waistline, you have the option of using one fastening for both, usually a zipper.

Finally, note whether your design includes petticoats. If so, you will need to plan how they will close, which will depend upon the corselette length.

Corselette fastenings

Zippers

Zippers are a simple, effective closure and can be placed in the centre back, side or centre front seam, usually in a centred application. To allow room for dressing, they are often longer than the corselette, opening to the low hip, while the corselette finishes at the waist or high hip. The extra length can be attached to the skirt lining or petticoat, or left to hang loose inside the garment. The corselette zipper is generally sewn by machine and set 1cm or 2cm (⅜" or ¾") below the top edge, allowing space for a hook and eye.

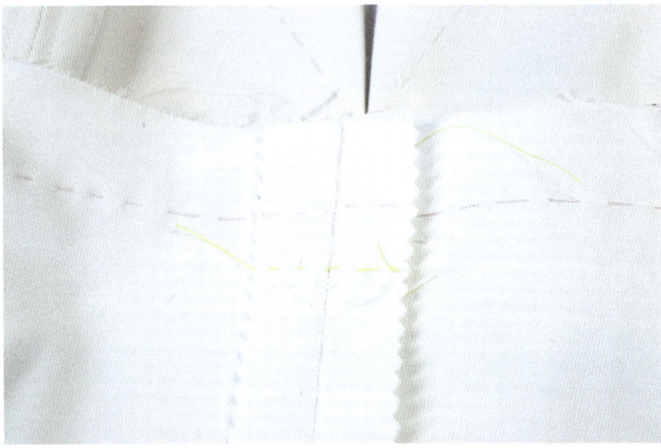

Figure 9.1

Attaching a centred zipper

1. Baste the zipper seam then press it open. Mark the zipper top (Figure 9.1).

Figure 9.2

2. Open the zipper. Place it face down on the seam allowance only, placing the zipper top at the upper mark and the zipper teeth next to the seamline (Figure 9.2). Angle the zipper tape slightly into the seam allowance at the top. Baste in place, keeping the corselette free. The excess zipper length will extend below the lower edge.

3. Fold the seam allowances to the corselette and baste through all layers 6mm (¼") from the zipper teeth (Figure 9.3).

Figure 9.3

4. From the right side, use a zipper foot to sew along the basting through all thicknesses (Figure 9.4). Remove the basting. Attach a hook and eye above the zipper once the upper edge of the corselette is finished.

Figure 9.4

Hooks and eyes

Hooks and eyes provide a secure, flat closure which holds up well under tension. They can be applied in any seam, although they are difficult (if not impossible) for the wearer to fasten when they are placed at the centre back. Typically, the hooks are placed on the right-hand side of the opening, or on the front section if they are in the side seam. They can be faced away from the body, but when they face inwards, an extension can be added to protect the wearer from any discomfort. A length of boning on one or both sides of the opening will help support the area, as well as making it easier to fasten. Hooks and eyes can be attached on a pre-made tape or sewn on individually.

Hook and eye tape

Using ready-made hook and eye tape is a quick alternative to sewing them on one-by-one. There are several ways to attach hook and eye tape; however, the following method gives a neat finish while hiding the hooks and creating a boning channel. Use a zipper foot, taking care to avoid the metal.

Figure 9.5

Applying hook and eye tape

1. Mark the centre back seamline and the upper and lower edges of the tape (Figure 9.5).

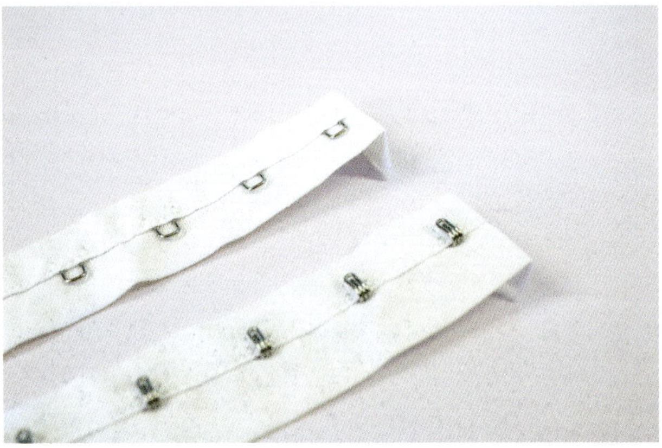

Figure 9.6

2. Cut the required length of hook and eye tape and fold under the raw edges on the cut ends (Figure 9.6).

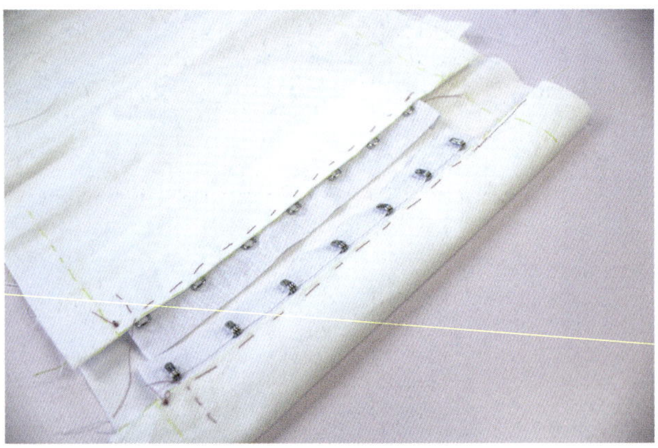

Figure 9.7

3. Fold under the centre back seam allowances. Place the left back over the eye tape with the eyes extending 3mm (⅛") past the seamline. Next, place the right back over the hook tape, matching the positions of the eyes. Set the head of the hook just next to the foldline. Baste both in place (Figure 9.7).

4. Stitch down both sides close to the fold line, sewing from edge to edge (Figure 9.8).

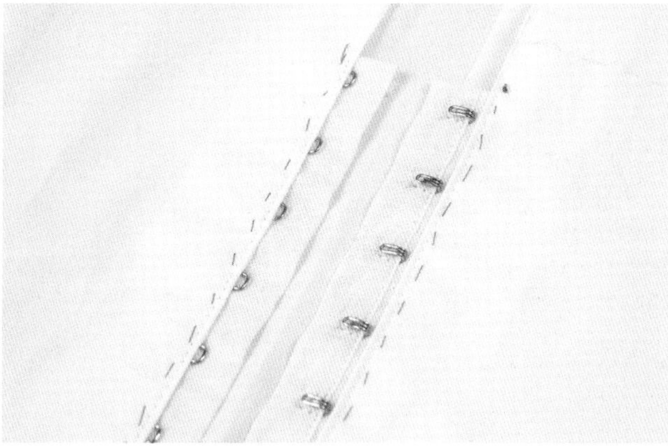

Figure 9.8

> ## TIP
>
> If the spacing of the hooks and eyes on your tape does not match the length of your corselette opening, position the top hook and eye 3mm below the upper seamline, and then hand sew an extra hook and eye set at the lower edge.

5. Fold the tapes to the inside. Baste in place then sew 1cm (⅜") from the first row of stitching (Figure 9.9). This secures the tape and creates a channel which can house a bone if you wish (Figure 9.10).

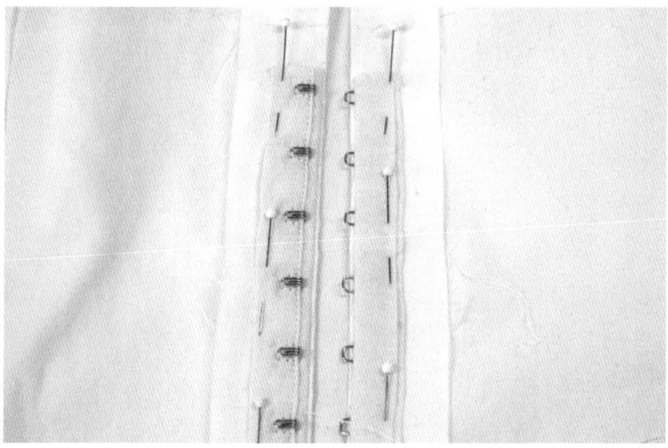

Figure 9.9

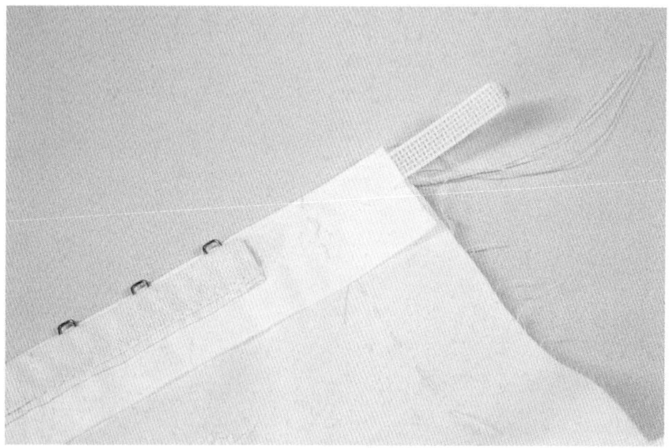

Figure 9.10

Adding a fabric extension

1. Cut a rectangle of corselette fabric 8cm (3⅛") wide and the length of the finished opening, plus seam allowances. Fold it in half lengthwise with the right sides together and sew the two short edges. Turn right side out and press (Figure 9.11).

Figure 9.11

2. Place the extension behind the eyes, leaving a 1.5cm (⅝") overhang. Machine stitch it to the seam allowance on the inner edge (Figure 9.12).

Figure 9.12

3. Slipstitch it at the centre back between the eyes (Figure 9.13).

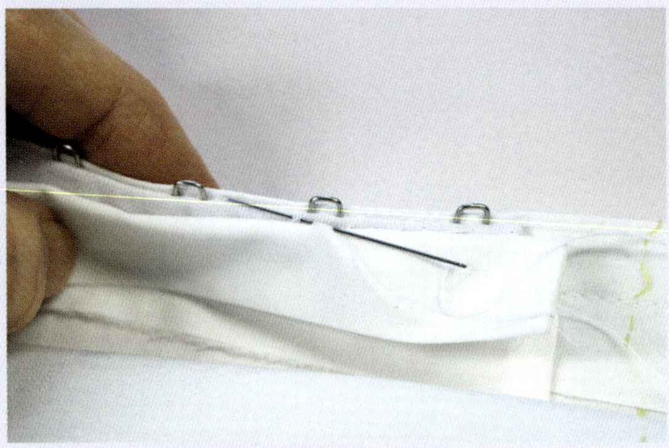

Figure 9.13

Individual hooks and eyes

While more time-consuming, sewing on individual hooks and eyes gives you control over their position and spacing. The hooks are usually attached to one side of the opening and the eyes to the other, but they can be alternated to give an even more secure closure. The opening is strengthened with tape and can be further reinforced with rows of stitching or supported with boning.

Creating a hook and eye closure

1. On the wrong side, baste a length of 1.5cm-wide (⅝"-wide) twill tape next to the centre back seamline.
2. Fold the seam allowance inside over the tape and stitch in place close to the fold and again 1cm (⅜") from the stitching, securing the tape. This also creates a boning channel (Figure 9.14).

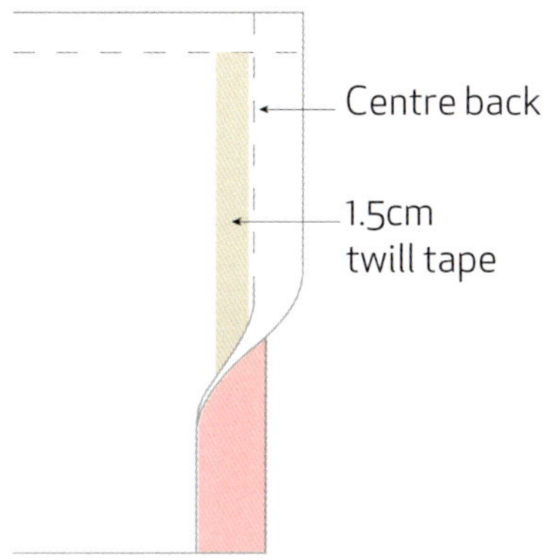

Figure 9.14

3. Sew the hooks to the right back, placing the hooks 3mm (⅛") in from the fold with the upper and lower hooks 3mm (⅛") in from the seamline. Space the remaining hooks 2cm–2.5cm (¾"–1") apart. Sew through the seam allowance and tape only (Figure 9.15).
4. On the left back, mark the placement for the eyes opposite the hooks. Position the eyes 3mm (⅛") over the fold. Attach the eyes, sewing through the seam allowance and tape only.

For firm support, boning can be inserted into one or both channels.

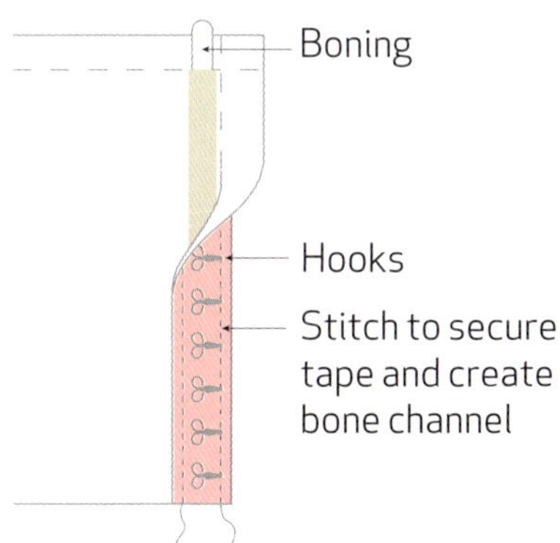

Figure 9.15

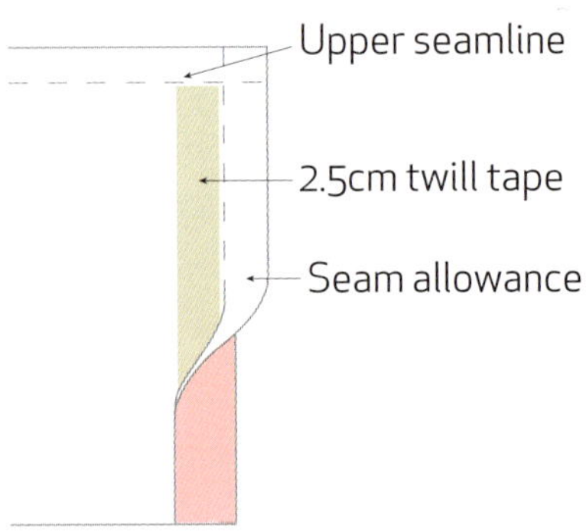

Figure 9.16

If more gentle reinforcement is preferred, the opening can instead be stiffened with multiple rows of stitching. The process is similar, but begins with a wider tape.

1. Cut lengths of 2.5cm-wide (1"-wide) twill tape to fit the length of the opening between the upper seamline and the lower edge, basting them on the wrong side next to the centre back seamline (Figure 9.16).

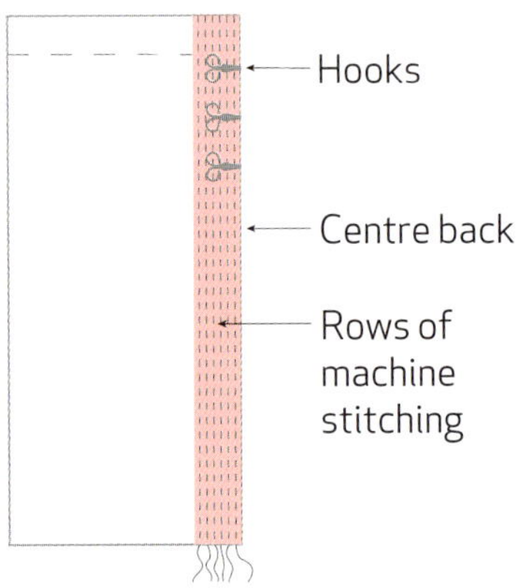

Figure 9.17

2. Fold the seam allowance inside over the tape, and stitch 3mm (⅛") from the folded edge. Continue with rows of stitching 3mm (⅛") apart to the edge of the tape (Figure 9.17).
3. Continue with Steps 3 and 4 above.

TIP

For strength, use a double waxed thread when attaching hooks and eyes.

Concealing hooks and eyes

Hooks and eyes may be left visible, but usually they are hidden for a clean finish. In a lined corselette they are covered by the lining, while in an unlined corselette they can be covered with tape or ribbon, or a fabric facing can be applied during construction.

Lining

Turn in the closure seam allowances of the lining along the seamline. Place the left-side folded edge over the eyes, aligning it with the edge of the corselette, and the right-side folded edge close up under the hooks. Slipstitch the lining to the corselette along both edges (Figure 9.18).

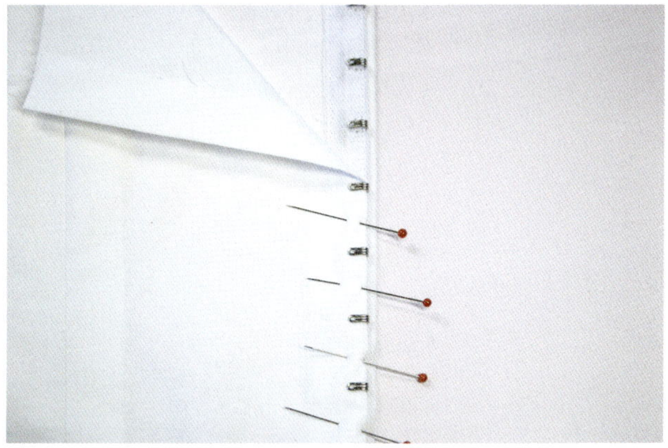

Figure 9.18

Tape or ribbon

This is an ideal finish for a double-layer corselette, where the tape can be hand sewn to the inner layer only. Suitable choices for this technique include Petersham or grosgrain, satin or taffeta ribbon or seam binding of around 1.5cm (⅝") in width. Cut a length of ribbon to fit the opening, plus 2cm (¾"). Turn in the short ends and position over the hooks and eyes as described for a lining. Slipstitch the ribbon in place around all edges (Figure 9.19).

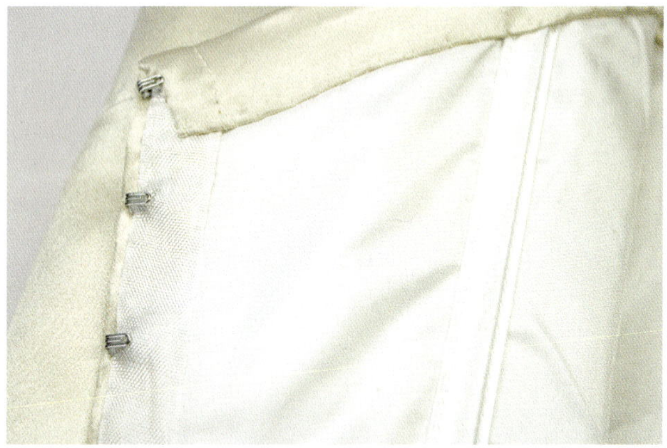

Figure 9.19

A wider tape can also be placed behind the eyes, forming an extension to protect the wearer from the hooks. Petersham or grosgrain ribbon is best for this purpose, as these are firm enough to hold their shape. Cut a length of 2.5cm-wide (1"-wide) ribbon to fit the opening then bind the ends with seam binding, or overcast them to prevent unravelling. Place the tape behind the eyes, allowing an overhang. Slipstitch the tape to the corselette between the eyes and along the inside edge (Figure 9.20).

Figure 9.20

Fabric facing

A fabric facing can be used to conceal the hooks and eyes on a single- or double-layer corselette, and is attached as one of the first steps when installing the fastening.

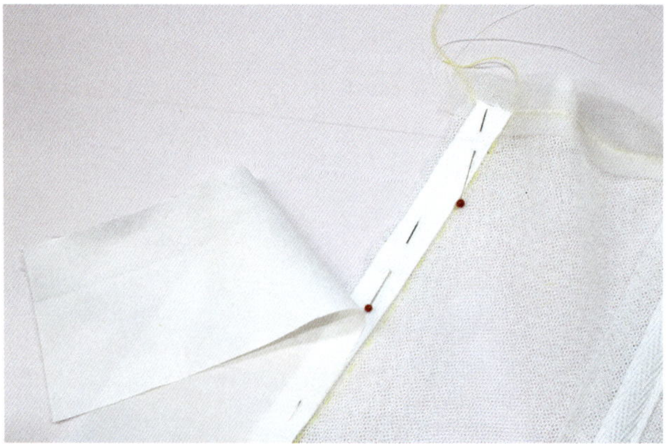

Figure 9.21

Applying a fabric facing

1. Cut two pieces of fabric the length of the opening and 7.5 cm (3") wide (the corselette or dress lining fabrics are often good choices) and two lengths of Petersham ribbon or twill tape to fit the length of the opening between the seamlines.
2. With the wrong side of the corselette facing you, place the tape on the seam allowance, aligning the tape edge with the centre back seamline. Next, position the facing over the tape (Figure 9.21).

Figure 9.22

3. Fold the seam allowances to the inside, baste them in place then stitch 3mm (⅛") from the folded edge. Finish the closure by either stitching again 1cm (⅜") away to create a boning channel or reinforcing the tape with multiple rows of stitching (Figure 9.22). (See 'Creating a hook and eye closure', page 85–6.)

Figure 9.23

4. Attach the hooks and eyes (Figure 9.23).

5. Turn in 1cm (⅜") on the facing edges then fold again, placing the facing under the hooks and over the eyes. Slipstitch it in place (Figure 9.24).

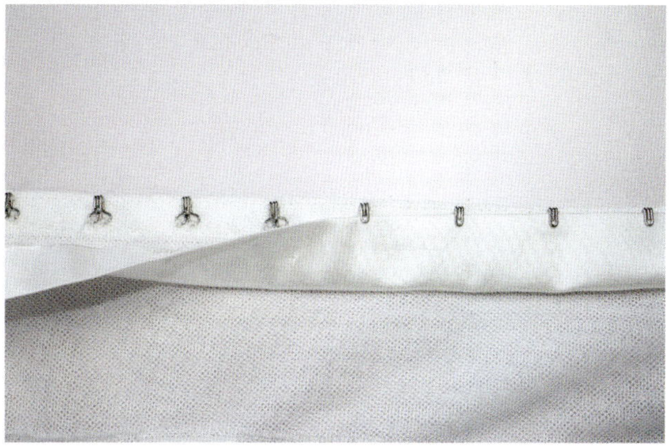

Figure 9.24

Waist stays

A waist stay, also known as an inside belt, anchors a garment firmly at the waistline (Figure 9.25). In a corselette it has a number of roles, including:

- Taking stress off the closure at the waistline.
- Supporting the weight of the skirts and petticoats.
- Anchoring the bodice and boning at the waistline to prevent it being dragged down or shifting.
- Making it easier to close the garment.

Waist stays are usually made from 2.5cm-wide (1"-wide) grosgrain or Petersham ribbon and are the measurement of the wearer's waistline or just slightly smaller to ensure that they are held snugly against the body. They are placed along the corselette waistline and attached to the bone casings, stopping 2.5cm (1") from the closure.

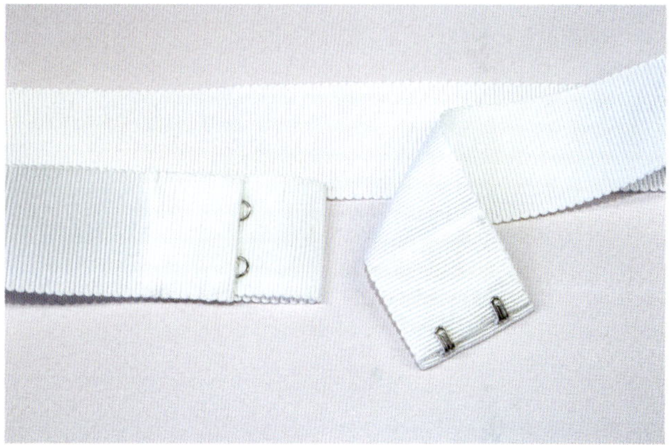

Figure 9.25

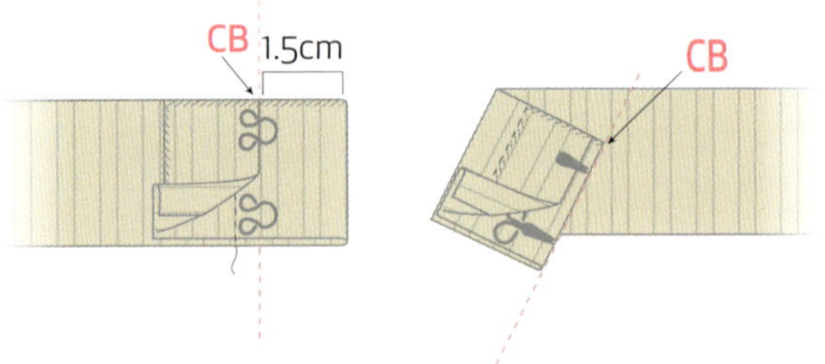

Figure 9.26

TIP

The stay can be fastened with two small hooks and eyes, or a single trouser or skirt hook and bar set.

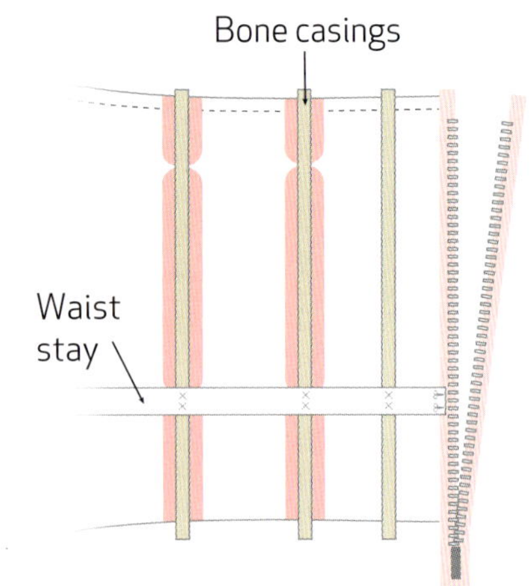

Figure 9.27

Making a waist stay

1. Cut a length of Petersham ribbon the required length plus 12.5cm (5").
2. On the hook end, turn under 5cm (2") and stitch through both layers 2cm (¾") from the fold. Stitch two small hooks to the end, setting them back 3mm (⅛") from the folded edge. Turn in the raw edge and slip under the hooks. Stitch around the outer edge to secure.
3. On the eye end, mark the centre back then fold 6cm (2⅜") to the outside. This creates a 1.5cm (⅝") extension past the waistline measurement. Machine stitch through both layers 2cm (¾") from the fold. Attach the eyes opposite the hook positions so they extend 3mm (⅛") past the centre back line. Turn in the raw edge and place over the eyes. Stitch around the outer edge to secure (Figure 9.26).

Attaching the waist stay

Match the centre of the waist stay with the centre front of the corselette. Place the lower edge of the waist stay on the corselette waistline and pin in place at each seam. Using a waxed thread, sew the waist stay firmly to the corselette at each boning channel or machine stitch it along both long edges between boning channels. Leave it free for approximately 2.5cm (1") from each end (Figure 9.27).

Skirt and petticoat fastenings

Due to differences in ease, a skirt or petticoat can't be joined to the fastening of a hip-length corselette. A skirt (even a slim-fitting one) or petticoat has ease, whereas the corselette does not, and attaching them will anchor the skirt to the body and interfere with its movement. Instead, skirts and petticoats need their own method of fastening.

Petticoat fastenings

When constructing a hip-length corselette, petticoats are generally hand sewn to the corselette after they are both completed. The petticoat is attached at or just below the waist and will have a closure of its own, usually a hemmed opening, to lie discreetly beneath the outer skirt (Figure 9.28).

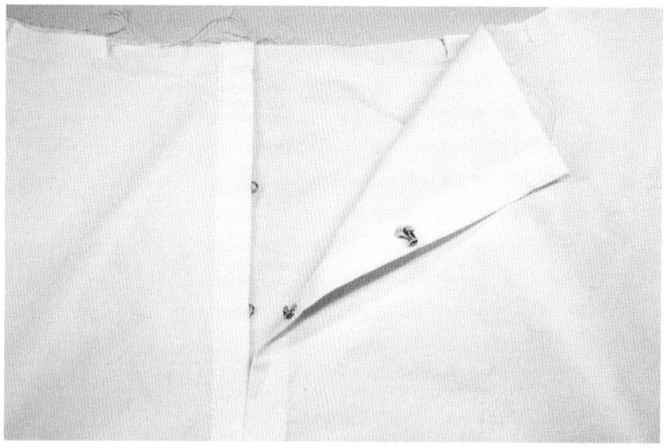

Figure 9.28

Skirt fastenings

When the outer garment has its own closure, it's likely that the fastening will extend into the skirt. However, when the corselette and the garment bodice share a single fastening, the skirt needs a separate closure to allow it to move freely around the body. In this situation, the skirt is finished, complete with the closure and lining (if applicable), before it is attached to the bodice. To close the garment skirt, use one of the following:

- A zipper.
- Buttons with buttonholes or loops.
- A concealed placket with snaps or hooks and eyes.
- A hemmed opening.

Creating a hemmed opening

A hemmed opening is a simple closure that is suitable for petticoats, full gathered skirts or where the opening is hidden under a pleat.

1. Mark the seamline in the opening and trim the seam allowance to 1.5cm (⅝"). Sew the seam from the lower edge to the beginning of the opening. Press the seam open.
2. Above the opening, turn under the seam allowances twice and stitch close to the inner fold.
3. Sew two or three hooks and eyes on the wrong side of the slit so that the edges meet when closed (Figure 9.29).

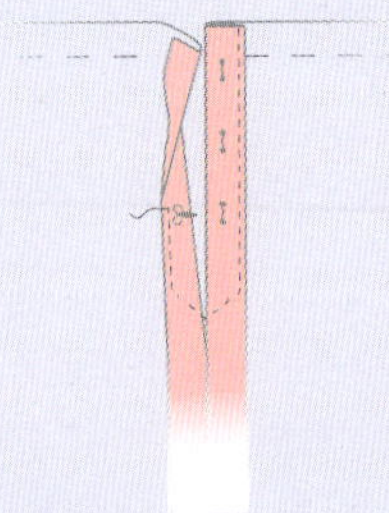

Figure 9.29

Creating a concealed placket

A concealed placket has an underlay which houses the fastening inconspicuously. It's useful when a visible fastening would spoil the appearance of the design. The placket will lap right over left at centre back, and front over back if placed at the side seam. For this technique, the skirt should be underlined, and wider seam allowances are used.

Creating the placket

1. Cut the skirt and underlining leaving 5cm-wide (2"-wide) seam allowances for the placket. Baste the underlining to the skirt pieces. On the underlap, mark a foldline for the extension 2cm (¾") from the seamline. Stitch the seam below the marking for the placket. Staystitch the upper edge and finish the seam allowances (Figure 9.30).

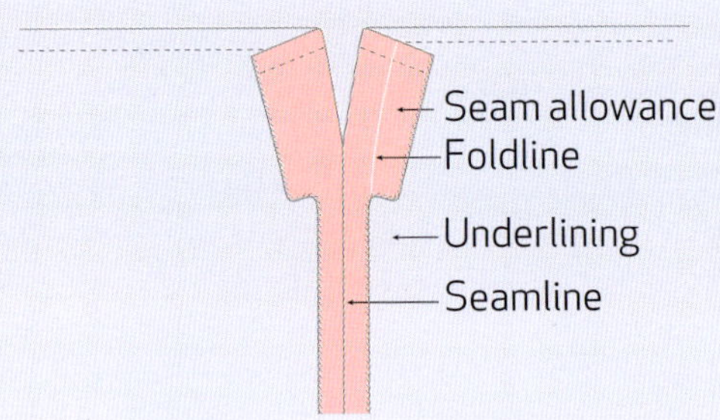

Figure 9.30

2. To create the underlap, fold the seam allowance on the foldline, right sides together. At the upper edge, stitch from the seamline to the fold. Clip to the seamline then turn out (Figure 9.31).

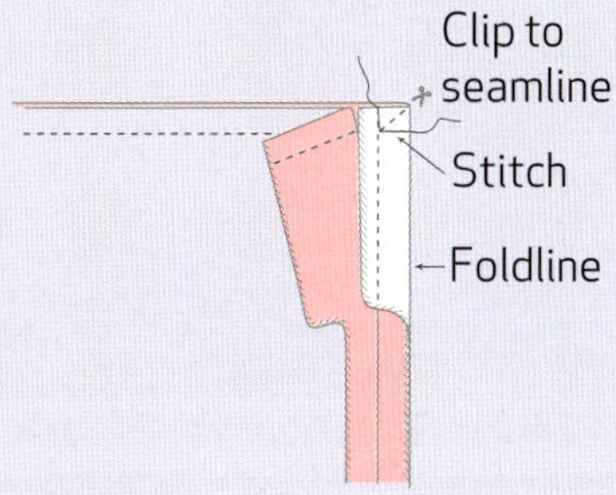

Figure 9.31

3. On the inside, stitch the lower edge of the extension to the seam allowance, keeping the skirt free (Figure 9.32).
4. To create the overlap, fold the seam allowance to the inside, catchstitching it in place.

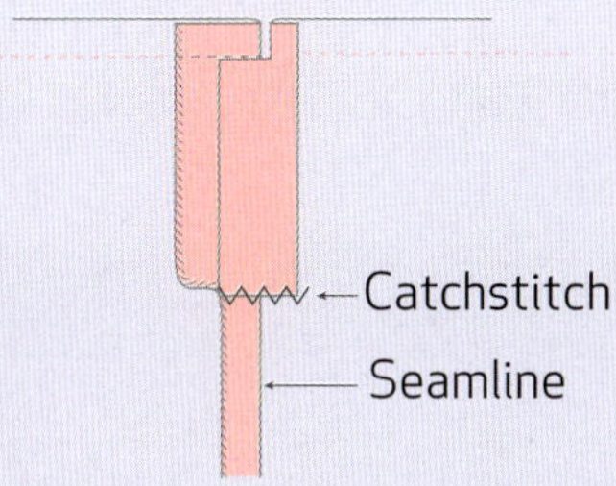

Figure 9.32

5. Sew snaps or hooks and eyes to the placket 3mm (⅛") inside the seamline. On the overlap, stitch through all layers except the outer one (Figure 9.33).

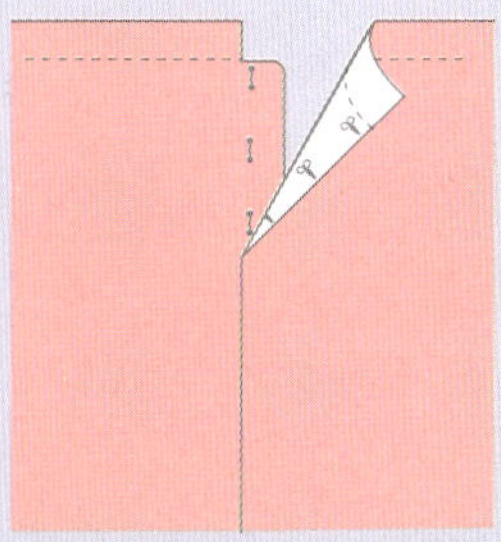

Figure 9.33

10

Joining the Inner Corselette and the Garment

Joining your corselette to the garment is an exciting step, as you watch your project finally come together. While this is the last step in the process, it is important to decide in the planning stage how you will join your corselette and garment, as your choice will affect the construction. There are two main methods used to join an inner corselette to its outer garment: machine sewing to the garment upper edge or hand sewing to the body of the garment. These options are very much determined by the design and fit of your garment.

Machine sewing to the garment upper edge

This method is easier to implement as only the upper edges of the corselette and the outer garment need to match exactly. As the upper edge is the only anchor point between the two, either a waist- or a hip-length corselette will work. Remember that the entire weight of the outer garment will be suspended from the upper edge, which makes this technique more suited to light to medium-weight outer garments. There are several situations when this joining method is suitable:

- When the upper edge of the outer garment and the inner corselette share the same shape and circumference.
- When there are no horizontal seams in the outer garment which the corselette can be anchored to (for example an empire or waist seam).
- When the outer garment is a semi-fitted or loose-fitting style such as a trapeze or shift dress.

There are two methods you can use to join the garment and the corselette by machine.

Faced method

Finishing the upper edge with a facing will cover the seam allowances and provide a continuity from the garment to the inside of the corselette. All seam allowances are drawn to the inside, providing more of a buffer and less chance of them being seen from the outside of the garment. This method can be used for a lined or an unlined garment.

Sew the corselette

Assemble the corselette shell using your choice of methods and add the bone casings and boning. Finish the lower edge and install the fastening 2cm (¾") below the upper seamline, leaving the upper edge unfinished. Staystitch and stabilize the upper edge (Figure 10.1).

Figure 10.1

Sew the garment

1. Construct the outer garment. Install the zipper 1cm (⅜") below the upper seamline, leaving the upper edge unfinished.
2. Sew the garment lining together. Slip the lining into the garment, wrong sides together. Baste together along the upper seamlines and slipstitch the lining to the zipper tape (Figure 10.2).

Figure 10.2

Figure 10.3

Connect the layers

1. Slip the corselette into the garment with the right side of the corselette facing the lining. Match the upper seamlines and baste together (Figure 10.3).

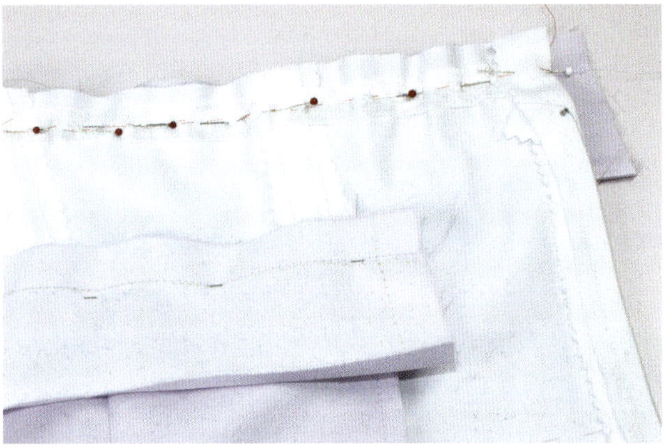

Figure 10.4

Add the facing

1. Prepare the facing and place it right sides together with the garment, matching the seamlines at the upper edge. Stitch through all layers. Trim and grade the seam allowance (Figure 10.4).
2. Turn the facing to the inside. Understitch, keeping the garment and the lining free.

Figure 10.5

Finish the upper edge

1. Turn in the ends of the facing diagonally, fold under the lower edge and slipstitch to the corselette (Figure 10.5).
2. To keep the corselette from rolling out, prick stitch through all layers except the outer layer, 1cm (⅜") from the upper edge.
3. Sew a hook and eye at the top of the facing.

Construct a facing

If the outer design does not have a facing pattern, you can prepare one using the corselette pattern.

Prepare the pattern

1. Overlap the corselette front pattern pieces on the princess seam. Mark the facing with a finished width of 3cm–4cm (1¼"–1⅝"). Trace the pattern onto tissue paper, adding seam allowances (Figure 10.6).

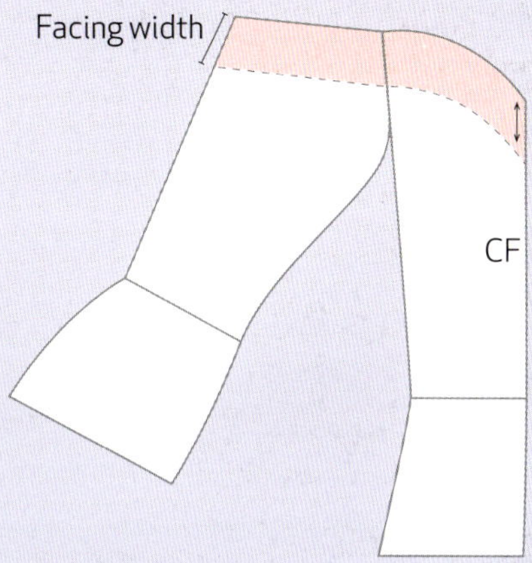

Figure 10.6

2. Repeat the process for the back.
3. Align the two facing pieces at the side seam and smooth the upper and lower curve between the front and back sections. Mark the grainline parallel to centre front and centre back (Figure 10.7).

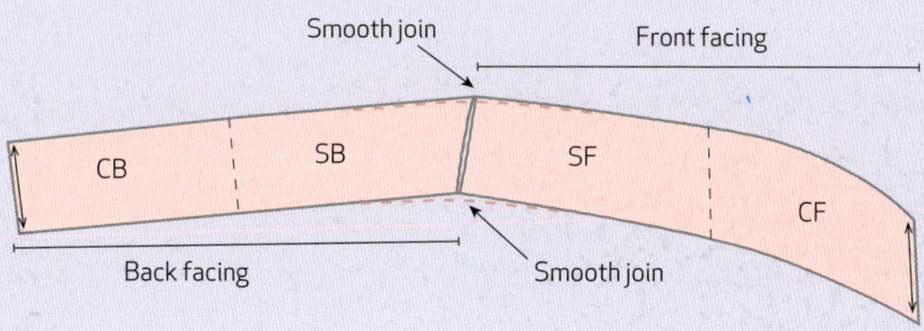

Figure 10.7

Sew the facing

1. Cut the facing pieces and apply a light interfacing.
2. Sew the facing together at centre front (or eliminate the seam and cut it on the fold). Sew the side seams. Trim the seams and press open.

Enclosed seam method

In this method the seam allowances are neatly hidden between the garment and the corselette, with a clean finish on the inside. It's best suited to a lined garment with a lined, woven (non-mesh) corselette.

Sew the corselette

Assemble the shell for a lined corselette. Add the boning channels, finish the lower edge and install the fastening. Place the boning into the casings. Staystitch across the upper edge of the main layer and stabilize it with tape. Baste the two layers together along the upper seamline.

Sew the garment

Construct the outer garment then add the fastening, leaving the upper edge unfinished. Sew the garment lining together, but do not join it to the garment.

Connect the layers

1. Place the wrong side of the corselette on the right side of the garment, matching the upper seamlines. Pin or baste together (Figure 10.8).
2. Next, place the lining and the garment rights sides together. The corselette will now be sandwiched between them. Baste first and then machine stitch through all layers between the centre back edges (Figure 10.9).

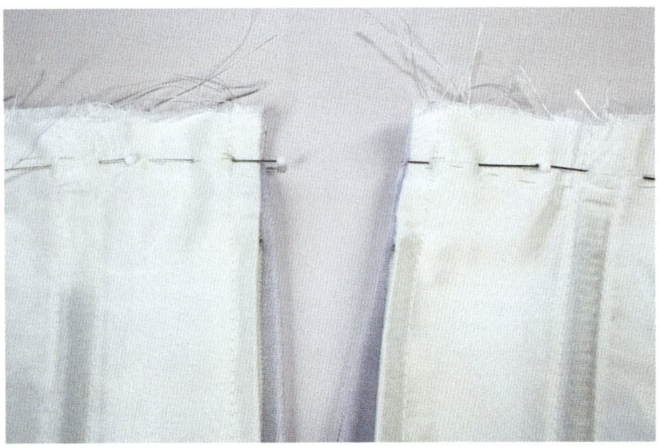

Figure 10.8

Figure 10.9

3. At the back opening, wrap the lining seam allowance to the inside, over the corselette and garment. Sew in place (Figure 10.10).
4. Trim, grade and clip the seam allowances as necessary. Turn the lining and corselette to the inside, enclosing the seam allowances.

Figure 10.10

Finish the upper edge

1. Understitch the upper edge by hand or machine, keeping the outer garment free (Figure 10.11).
2. Fold the lining under along the seamline on the opening edge and slipstitch to the zipper tape (Figure 10.12).
3. Attach a hook and eye above the zipper (Figure 10.13).

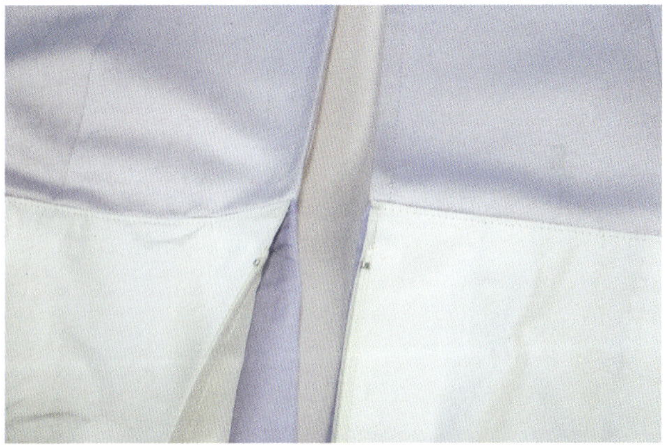

Figure 10.11

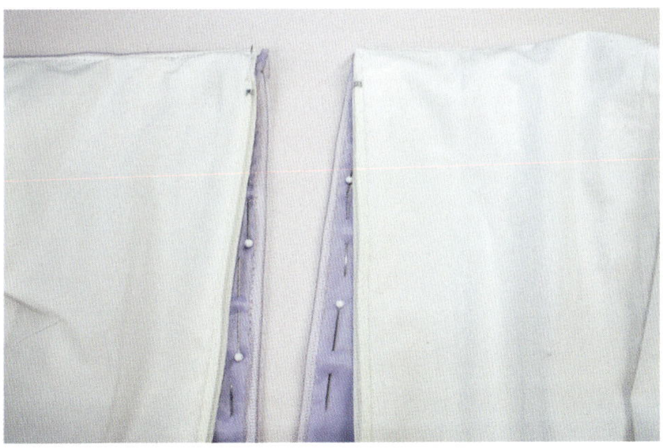

Figure 10.12

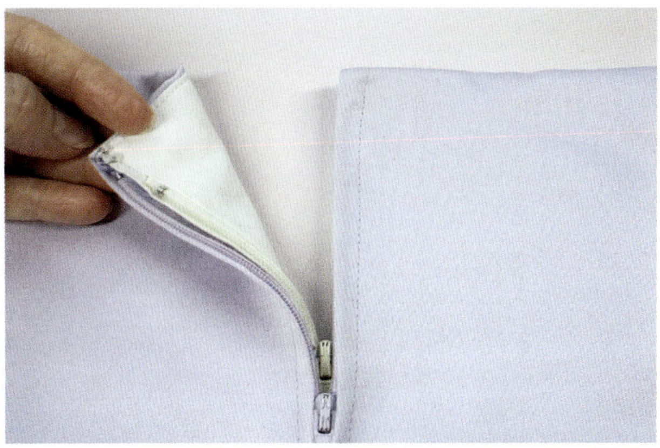

Figure 10.13

Hand sewing to the garment body

Hand sewing your corselette to the finished garment is a more challenging method as the two garments are connected at several points. It requires careful planning when creating your pattern to ensure that the match points of the two garments line up. An advantage of this technique is that it doesn't rely on the garment and corselette upper edges matching in design and fit. Additionally, with the garment and the corselette also secured through horizontal seamlines, more support is given to the outer design. For this method the bodice must have one or more horizontal seams and generally a hip-length corselette will work best.

This method is suitable for several garment designs:

- When the garment bodice has a horizontal seam (such as an empire or waist seam) and has the same circumference as the corselette along that seamline.
- When the bodice has a surplice or other irregularly shaped upper edge.
- When the bodice neckline has more ease than the corselette.

When preparing your corselette pattern, you will need to mark placement lines for the horizontal seamlines of the outer garment, so that they can act as a guide when you join them. Transfer the seamline positions from the garment bodice to the corselette pattern. During the toile fitting, check that all placement lines on the two garments match.

There are three methods you can use to join the garment and the corselette by hand and the most suitable method for your project will mainly be determined by the design and fit of the bodice. I've described the process when two fastenings are used; however, the methods can be adapted for one fastening, in which case it is added after the corselette and the garment are connected, as the final step.

Tiered edges method

In this method, the corselette is set just below the upper edge of the bodice, to keep it hidden. It is suitable for most bodice designs but is particularly useful when the upper edge of the bodice is not continuous, for example in a surplice style, or when the upper edge of the bodice is shaped or curved, such as with a sweetheart design. The corselette and the garment are each completed with their fastenings added, then joined as the last step.

Prepare the pattern

1. Remove 1cm (⅜") from the upper edge of the corselette pattern. Transfer the placement of the bodice seamlines onto the corselette pattern (Figure 10.14).

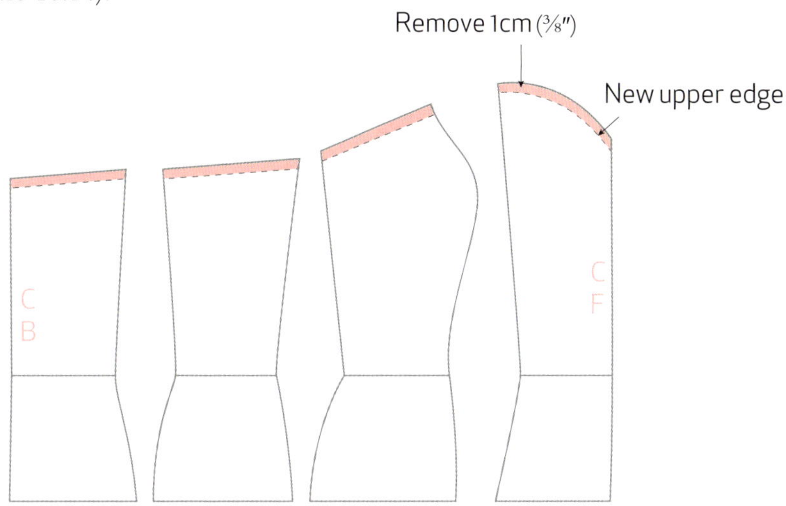

Figure 10.14

2. On the garment facing, mark a placement line for the corselette 1cm (⅜") below the upper edge (Figure 10.15).

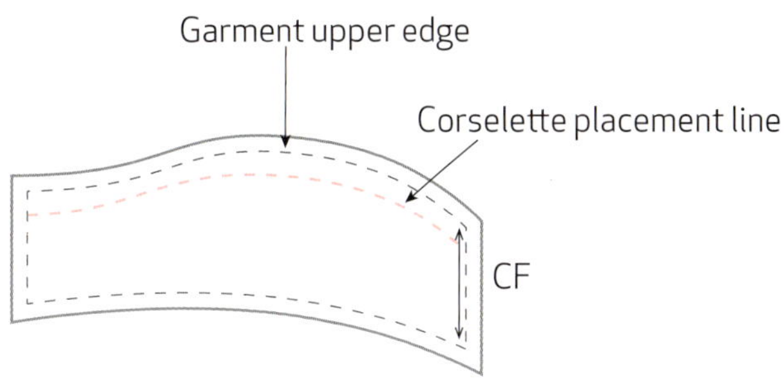

Figure 10.15

Complete the corselette

Be sure to thread trace the placement lines for matching with the bodice seams. A facing or a clean finish are the most suitable methods for finishing the upper edge. Install the fastening and attach petticoats if applicable.

Figure 10.16

Complete the garment

On the facing, mark the position for the corselette placement. Stabilize and finish the upper edge, securing the facing to the underlining or seam allowances. Install the fastening (Figure 10.16).

Figure 10.17

Connect the layers

1. Slip the completed corselette into the garment, with the right side of the corselette facing the wrong side of the garment. Match the seamlines on the bodice with the placement lines on the corselette and pin in place. If there is more than one seam to match, begin with the lowest.
2. With the garment facing you, hand stitch through all layers along each placement line, keeping the stitches hidden in the seamline. Stop 2.5cm (1") each side of the closure (Figure 10.17).

3. Smooth the bodice over the corselette, matching the placement line on the bodice facing to the upper edge of the corselette (Figure 10.18).

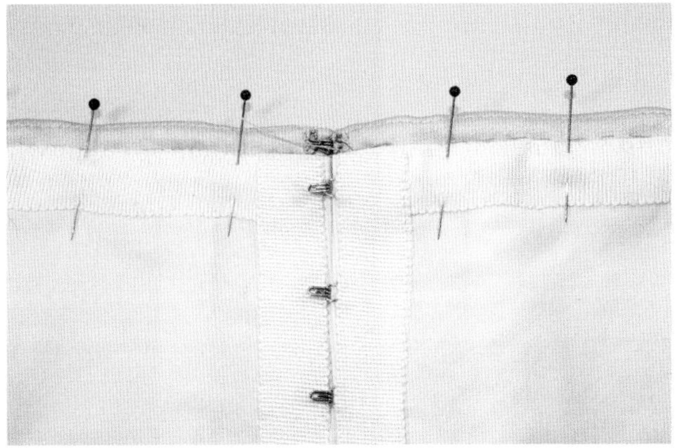

Figure 10.18

4. Slipstitch the corselette upper edge to the garment facing along the placement line, stopping 2.5cm (1") either side of the fastening (Figure 10.19).

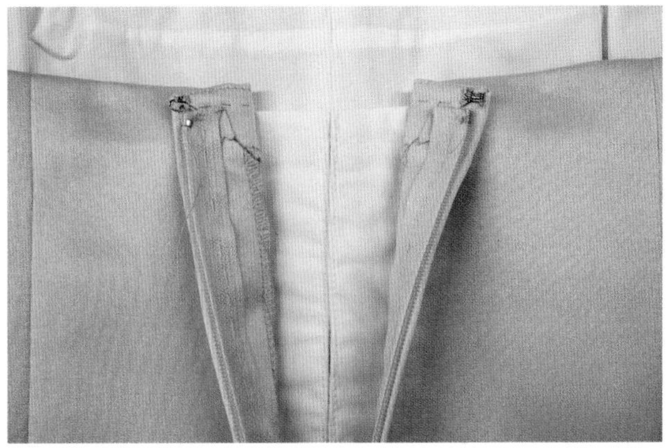

Figure 10.19

Wrapped edge method

When the upper edge of the garment has an extended facing, the corselette can be tucked underneath, hidden between the garment exterior and the facing. There are several design features which need to be met to use this method. Importantly, the design and fit of the garment and the corselette upper edges must match. In addition, the garment bodice must be underlined and the upper edge needs to be continuous. As an extended facing is used, the fashion fabric must be suitable to be worn inside next to the body and a straight or gently curved upper edge will work best.

Prepare the pattern

Mark the upper edge of the corselette as a foldline (do not lower it) and add a 1cm (⅜") hem allowance. On the bodice pattern, mark the upper edge as a foldline and add a 3cm–4cm (1¼"–1⅝") extension above for the facing. Transfer the position of the bodice seamlines, which will be joined to the corselette, to the corselette pattern (Figure 10.20).

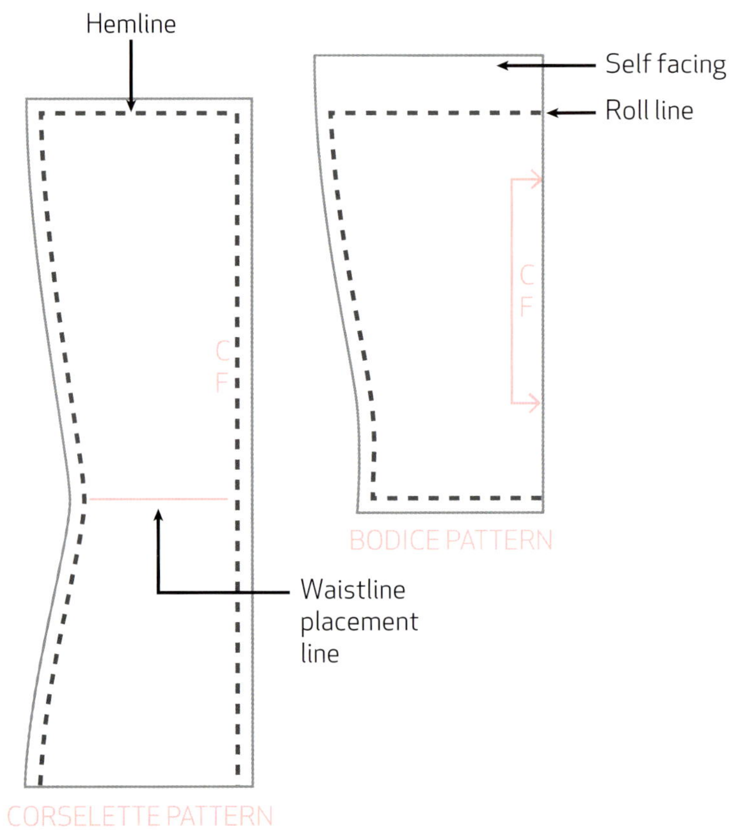

Figure 10.20

Sew the corselette

Sew the corselette shell, finish the upper and lower edges then add the fastening. To finish the upper edge, stabilize it with tape, turn it inwards on the foldline and catch-stitch it to the corselette (Figure 10.21).

Complete the garment

Sew the garment together, underlining the bodice. To prepare the upper edge, staystitch just outside the foldline and finish the raw edge to prevent unravelling. Install the fastening.

Figure 10.21

Connect the layers

1. Slip the corselette inside the garment. Smooth the garment over the corselette, matching the seamline to the placement line on the corselette. Stitch invisibly along the seamline through all layers, stopping 2.5cm (1") from the opening (Figure 10.22).

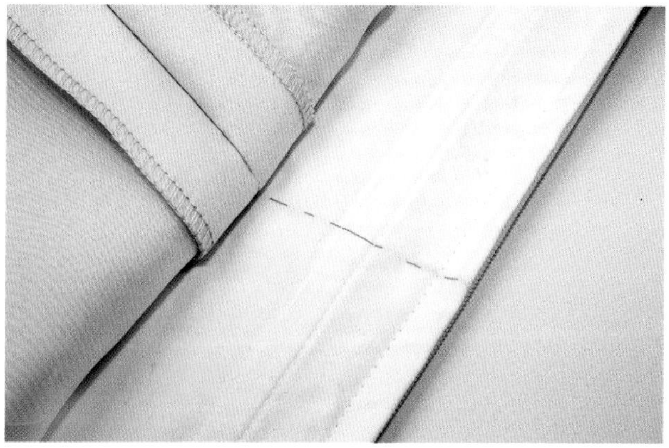

Figure 10.22

2. Place the upper edge of the corselette along the foldline of the garment. Slipstitch to the underlining only, so that it is invisible (Figure 10.23).

Figure 10.23

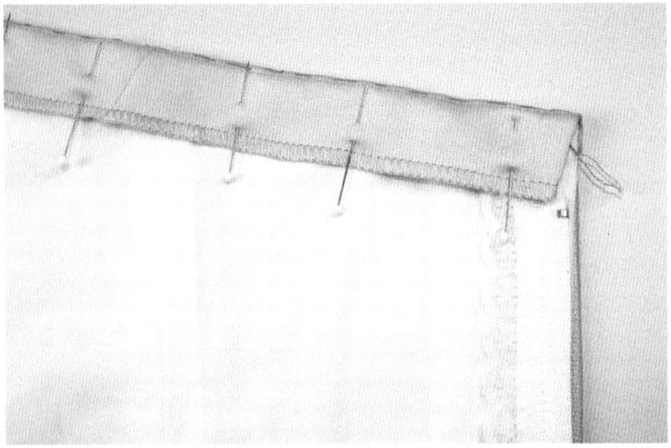

Figure 10.24

3. Fold the garment facing over the corselette. Turn in the ends at an angle at the opening. Catchstitch the facing to the corselette (Figure 10.24).

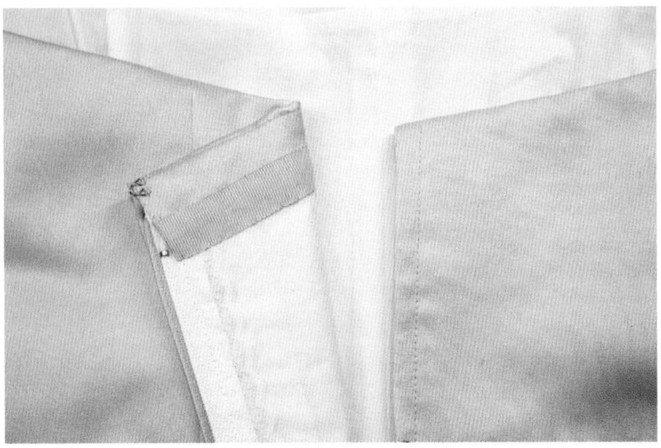

Figure 10.25

4. If desired, cover the lower edge of the facing with decorative tape or ribbon (Figure 10.25).

Floating edge method

When the garment upper edge has design ease, it is not possible to secure it closely to the corselette. In this case the garment and the corselette are connected through the bodice seamlines, and the upper edges are held together loosely with thread bars. A floating upper edge is desirable, for example, when the upper edge of the bodice includes fullness from pleats and ruffles or when there is a break in the line at the upper edge. It is also used when the corselette is supporting a garment with shoulders. As the garment and the corselette are loosely attached at the upper edge, the corselette is best bound with a fashion fabric as it will likely be seen.

Prepare the pattern

In a strapless design, the corselette is set just below the upper edge of the outer garment to keep it hidden. On the corselette pattern, remove 1cm (⅜") from the upper edge. Mark connection points for the bodice then mark the position of the thread bars. Thread bars are often best placed at the seams and near the edge of an opening, but should be positioned to suit the design (Figure 10.26).

On the garment pattern, mark the placement line for the corselette and the corresponding positions of the thread bars. For bodice designs with shoulders, check that the upper edge of the corselette will not be visible above the neckline or armhole and adjust the pattern if necessary.

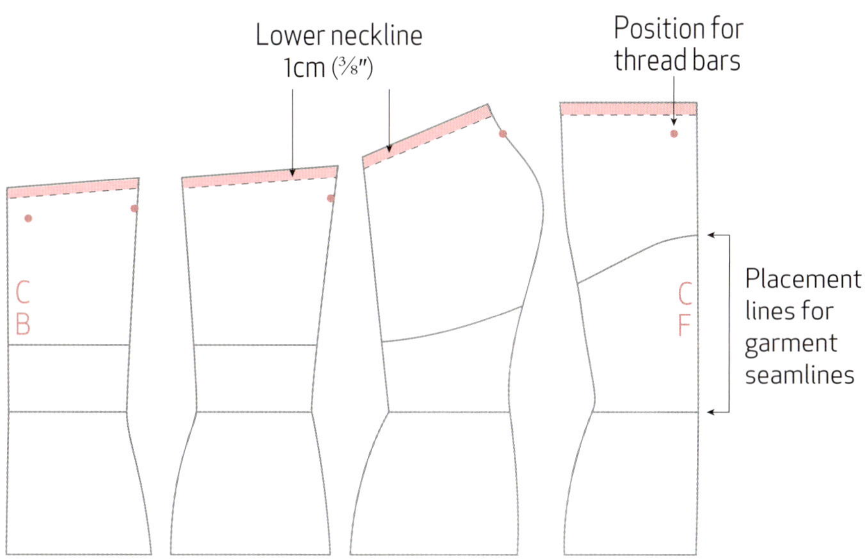

Figure 10.26

Figure 10.27

Complete the corselette

Sew the corselette, marking the placement line and thread bar positions. Complete the upper and lower edges and attach any petticoats before installing the fastening. A binding is a good choice for finishing the upper edge, which may be glimpsed as the two edges float freely (Figure 10.27).

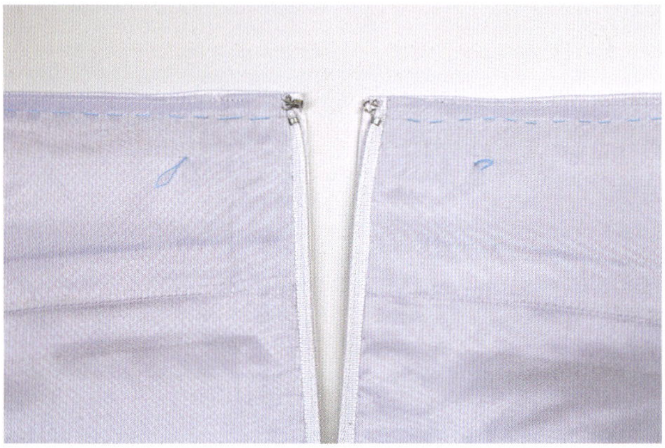

Figure 10.28

Complete the garment

Construct the garment and install the fastening. Stabilize the upper edge and finish it with a lining or facing. Ensure that the corselette placement line and the positions of the thread bars are clearly marked (Figure 10.28).

Figure 10.29

Connect the layers

1. Place the corselette inside the garment, matching the seamlines to the placement lines on the corselette. Sew invisibly along the seamlines through all layers, stopping 2.5cm (1") from the closure (Figure 10.29).

2. Smooth the garment over the corselette and match the upper edge of the corselette with the placement line on the garment (Figure 10.30).

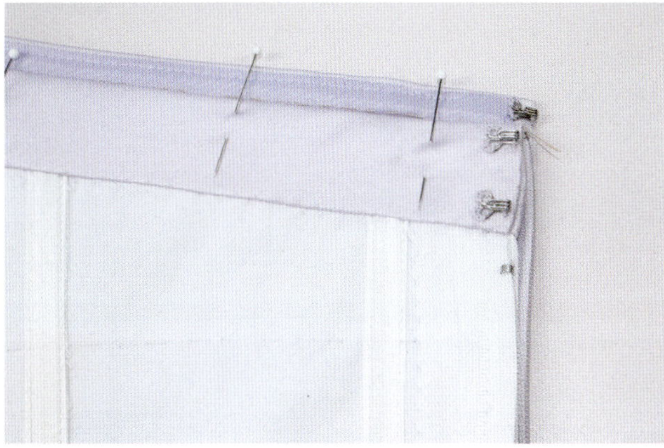

Figure 10.30

3. At the upper edge, join the two layers with French tacks (see 'Making a French tack (thread chain)', page 141) as required by the design (Figure 10.31).

Figure 10.31

CA 02776
100 m

Part Two

Applying the Techniques

As sewers, we all love to create! This part is about inspiring you to create beautiful designs of your own, incorporating an inner corselette. Each project showcases a range of skills and techniques demonstrating the use of different construction and joining methods, fabrics, boning and fastenings. Discover a variety of methods for developing the corselette pattern, ranging from simple to more advanced, and see how to adapt a readily available commercial pattern to create your own distinctive designs with an inner corselette. Use these projects to stimulate your imagination and creativity to experiment with different combinations of the techniques in your own work.

11

The Classic Mini Dress

Youthful and chic, the strapless shift has a minimalist silhouette that is easily taken from day to night by the choice of fabric. The style relies entirely on an inner corselette to anchor the dress to the body. A waist-length corselette provides a firm base, supporting the dress from the upper edge and allowing it to have a small amount of ease for comfort and movement.

This is a perfect project for those making an inner corselette for the first time. As the corselette pattern is provided with the dress pattern, there is no need to create one. The fitting process is also a little easier for a waist-length corselette. The classic lines in the dress allow a good fit to be achieved without much difficulty. Because of this we can really focus on the construction, learning how to use woven plastic boning, apply casings, install hook and eye tape and add a stay to support the waist. The dress is a slightly looser fit than the corselette, and has a separate fastening. We will see how to position the fastenings correctly and join the layers neatly along the upper edge with a ribbon facing.

Prepare the patterns

The Vogue evening pattern used for this project includes a waist-length corselette, making the preparation straightforward (there are generally commercial patterns available that include a corselette, which is a great way to begin). A simple reshaping of the front upper edge and shortening of the dress length creates the desired style.

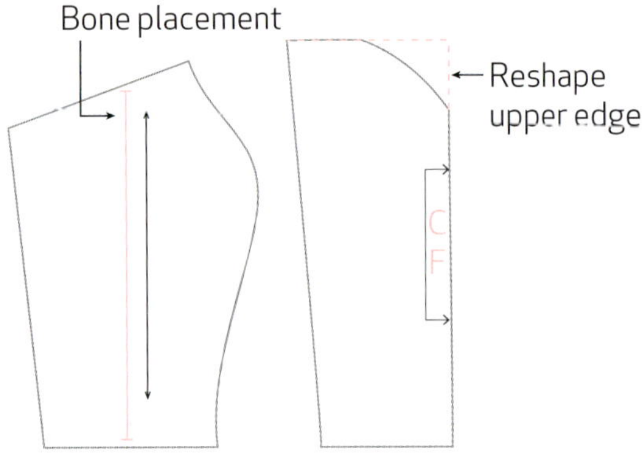

Figure 11.1

Prepare the corselette pattern

Trace the corselette pattern. Make any known adjustments required to fit the figure then mark the desired shape for the upper edge (Figure 11.1).

Prepare the dress pattern

Trace the dress pattern to the chosen length and reshape the upper edge to match the corselette. Copy any changes made to the fit of the corselette onto the dress pattern. An example would be a full bust adjustment or changes to the upper body length.

Sew and fit the toiles

To achieve the correct final fit, it is important to construct and fit toiles for both the corselette and the dress.

Fit the corselette toile first, adjusting it until it moulds to the figure. Check that the bust and waist levels match those of the wearer then decide where the bones need to be placed. In this case, they are placed on each seam and either side of the front princess seam as per the pattern instructions. Extra bones are also placed either side of the closure to add support at the centre back (Figure 11.2).

Once you are happy with the fit of the corselette toile, it is time to fit the dress toile. Make any adjustments needed for the figure. If you altered the upper edge of the corselette toile, remember to make the same adjustment to the upper edge of the dress. As they are joined along this edge, the circumferences and the style lines need to be the same.

Finally, fit both toiles together to determine how they will fit when worn. Pin the upper edges together, checking that they match (Figure 11.3). Ensure that the upper edge isn't too tight, as a little space is needed to accommodate the seam allowances and facing when they are turned in. The corselette should be snug while the dress has a small amount of ease. In this case, the dress has about 2.5cm (1") of ease at the waist and 5cm (2") at the hips.

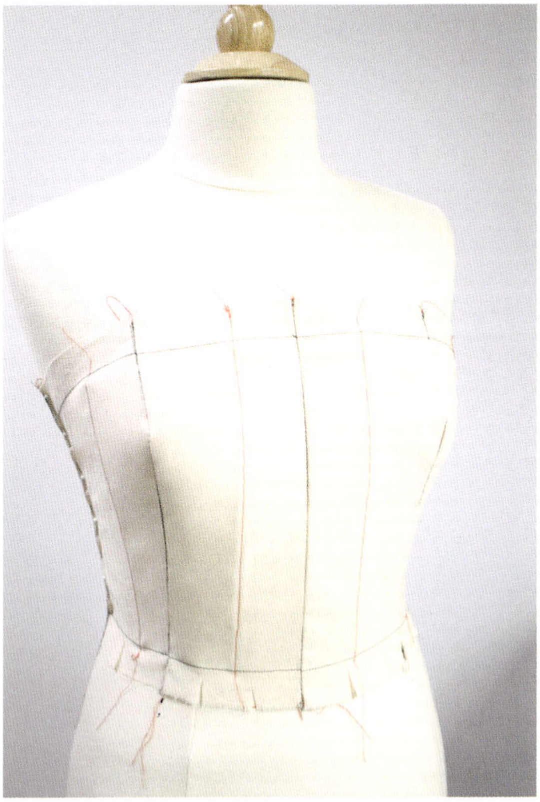

Figure 11.2

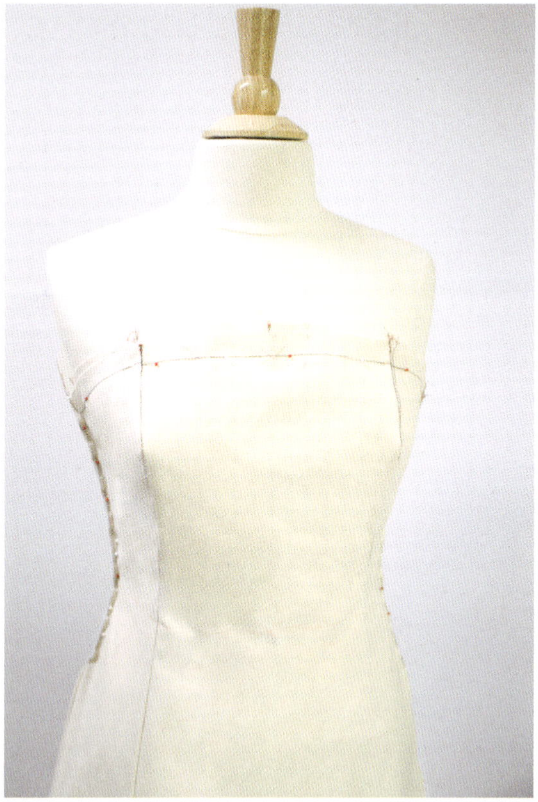

Figure 11.3

Construct the inner corselette

Two layers of a firmly woven cotton are used to construct the corselette, both cut on the same grain. It contains twelve woven plastic bones in cotton tape casings. Although this boning can be sewn to the fabric, placing it in a casing allows the corselette to be worked on without the boning, which is a little easier. The corselette closes with hook and eye tape. A simplified waist stay of Petersham ribbon finishes the lower edge and supports the corselette waistline (Figure 11.4).

The instructions provided with the pattern to construct the corselette are a useful starting point. We'll adapt them and use a unique combination of techniques.

Figure 11.4

Figure 11.5

Sew the corselette shell

Prepare the two corselette shells following the instructions for a lined corselette. It's easier to sew on the mid-panel casings now while the panels are still flat (Figure 11.5). In this case, the front princess seams are pressed towards the centre front, rather than open. This makes it easier to get a smooth result over the curve of the bust, particularly with woven boning. Press all other seams open. Set the lining aside until needed.

Figure 11.6

Add the bone casings

Working with the outer shell, position casings on the centre front panel next to the seamline, covering the seam allowance. Centre cotton tape over the remaining seams and bone placement lines. Measure the length for each bone and cut lengths to fit, then finish the ends. Check that the bones fit the casings properly, then set them aside until needed. It helps to have a fitting at this point, to check progress and make any further adjustments that may emerge (Figure 11.6).

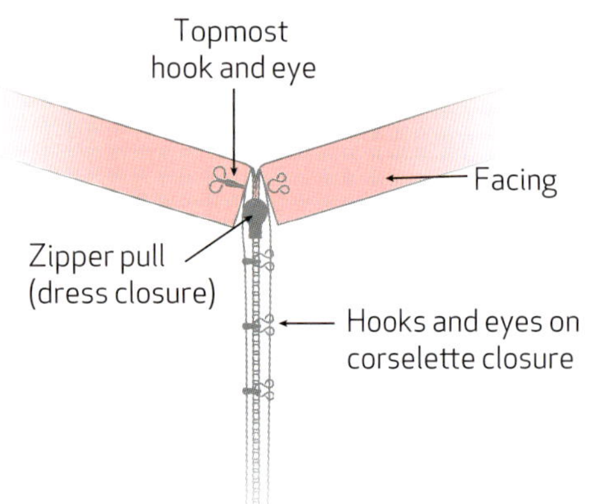

Figure 11.7

Positioning the hooks and eyes

When installing the closures of the corselette and dress, it is important to consider their respective positions when the garment is closed. It is not ideal to have them stacked up on each other creating unnecessary bulk. Topmost will be a hook and eye, then the zipper pull for the dress. Next is the corselette closure, which is best set below the zipper pull (Figure 11.7). Setting the corselette's top hook and eye 2cm (¾") below the upper edge positions it correctly.

Apply the hook and eye tape

Sew on the hook and eye tape (see pages 81–3), keeping it out of the lower seam allowance to reduce bulk (Figure 11.8). As the hooks face inwards, add an extension for the wearer's comfort, if desired (Figure 11.9).

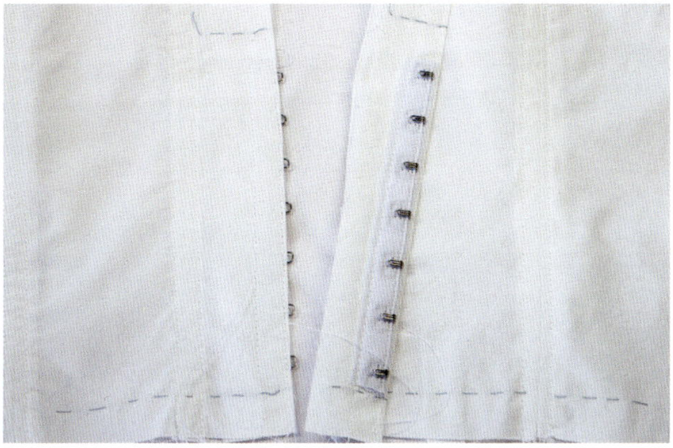

Figure 11.8

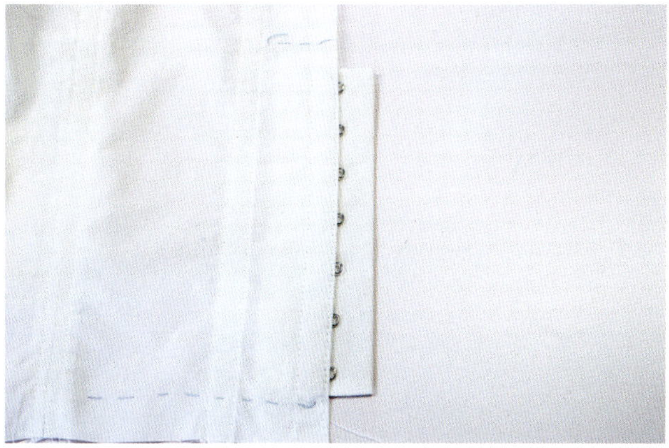

Figure 11.9

Finish the lower edge

The lower edge of the corselette has a clean finish with a length of Petersham ribbon along the waistline. This helps anchor the corselette and support the waistline, preventing it from stretching.

1. With right sides together, join the lining and the corselette at the lower edge. Trim the seam allowance and press it towards the lining.
2. With the right sides facing you, place a length of Petersham ribbon along the lower edge of the lining. Position the edge of the ribbon next to the seamline and allow it to overhang the centre back (Figure 11.10).

Figure 11.10

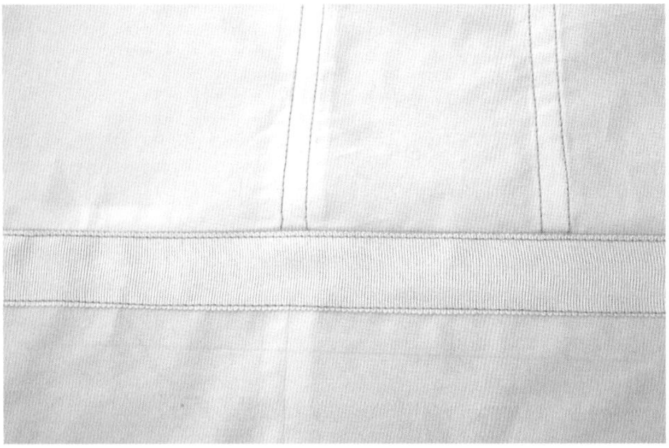

Figure 11.11

Figure 11.12

3. Stitch the ribbon to the lining along both edges (Figure 11.11). Turn the lining to the inside and press the lower edge.
4. With the right side of the corselette facing you, stitch along the bone casing, stitching at each seamline through all layers, securing the Petersham ribbon (Figure 11.12).

Figure 11.13

Add the boning

The corselette is almost completed now, and it is time for the finishing touches. Insert the boning into the casings and then staystitch across the upper seamline (Figure 11.13).

Finish the upper edge

Centre seam binding over the staystitching and stitch in place (Figure 11.14). Add hanging loops to the lining, basting them to the upper seamline at the side seams, then stitching again 3cm (1¼") below (Figure 11.15).

Figure 11.14

Figure 11.15

Join the lining

Turn the lining up and fold in the seam allowances on the back opening. Place the lining over the tape by slipping one edge under the hooks (Figure 11.16). Place the other edge over the extension, matching the centre back seamline behind the eyes. Slipstitch both in place. Join the lining and the corselette along the upper seamline and baste together (Figure 11.17).

TIP

Use pliers to open the lowest hook a little, if necessary, to clear the waist stay.

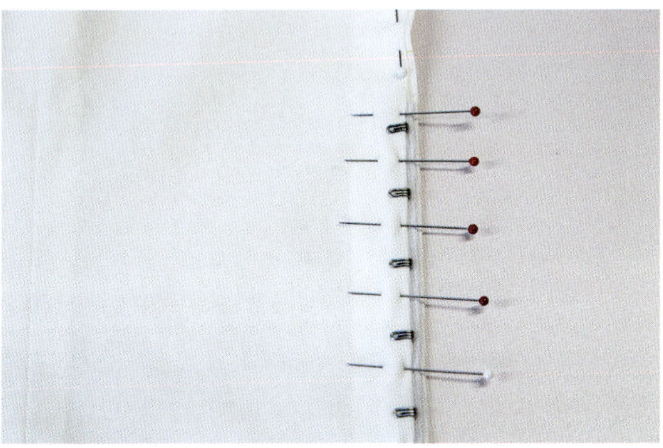

Figure 11.16

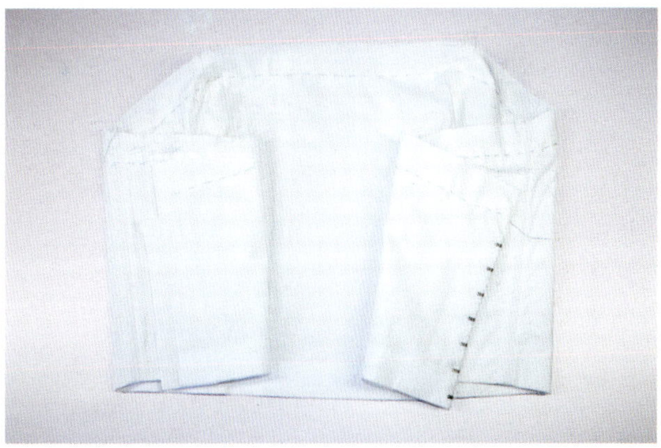

Figure 11.17

Sew the dress

With its close fit, this design is best suited to a fabric with some structure. Cotton piqué, a textured medium-weight fabric which holds its shape well, was selected as the fashion fabric. It is also easy to work with, making it a great choice when learning the techniques. The dress is lined and closes with an invisible zipper in the centre back. Ensure that any changes made to the fit of the upper edge of your corselette are transferred to your dress pattern so that they will match later when joining the two together.

Cut and sew the panels

After making any pattern adjustments from the toile fitting, cut the dress panels (Figure 11.18). Staystitch the upper edges then baste the panels together. Often some minor adjustments are needed in the fashion fabric, so it's a good idea to check the fit at this point. Baste the upper edge to the corselette for a fitting, make any final adjustments to the dress then sew the panels together. Trim and clip the seams as necessary, pressing them open to distribute their bulk evenly along the upper edge (Figure 11.19).

Figure 11.18

Figure 11.19

Add the zipper

Apply interfacing to the zipper area then machine or hand sew the zipper in place using a centred application. Set the top of the zipper 1cm (⅜") below the upper edge (Figure 11.20).

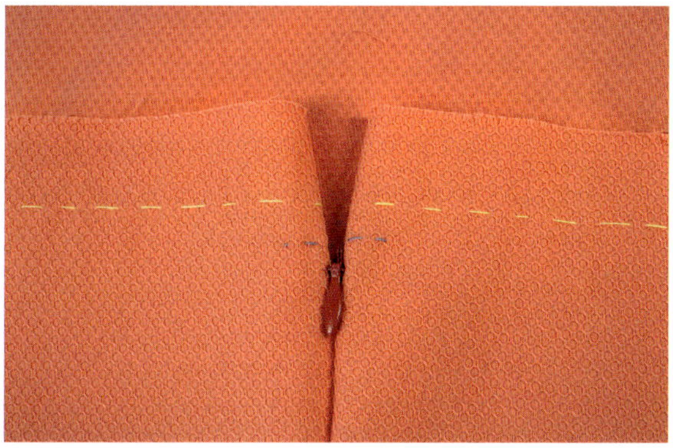

Figure 11.20

Sew and install the lining

Cut and prepare the lining panels in the same way as for the dress. Place the lining inside the dress, wrong sides facing (Figure 11.21). Baste the top edges together and slipstitch the lining to the zipper tape (Figure 11.22).

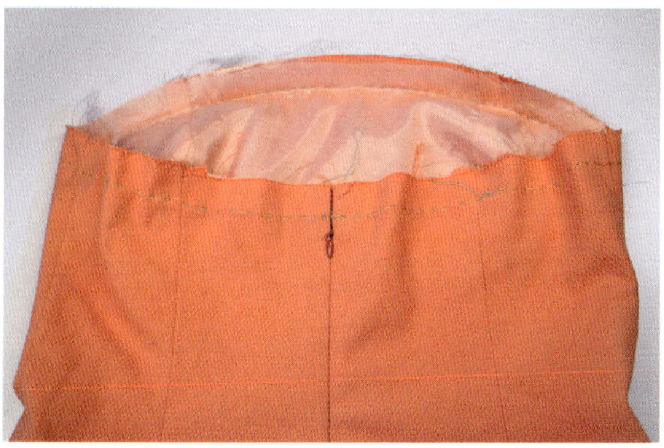

Figure 11.21

Figure 11.22

Join the inner corselette and dress

Now that the corselette and the dress are completed, they are ready to be joined. As the upper edge is fairly straight, it is possible to use a ribbon as the facing, eliminating the need to create a pattern.

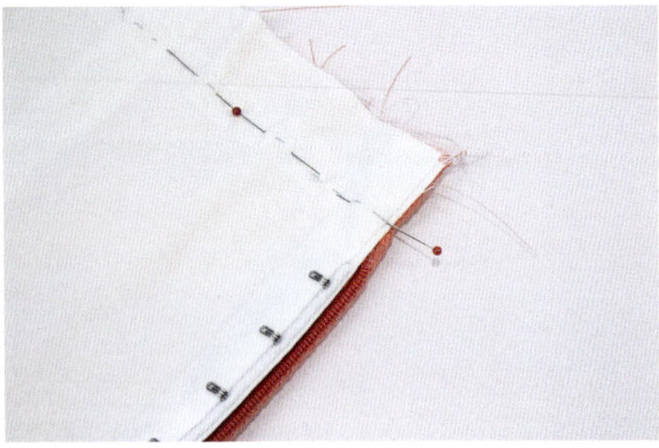

Figure 11.23

Attach the corselette

Slip the corselette into the lined dress, with the outside of the corselette (the layer with the boning) facing the dress lining. Match the upper seamlines and baste them together (Figure 11.23).

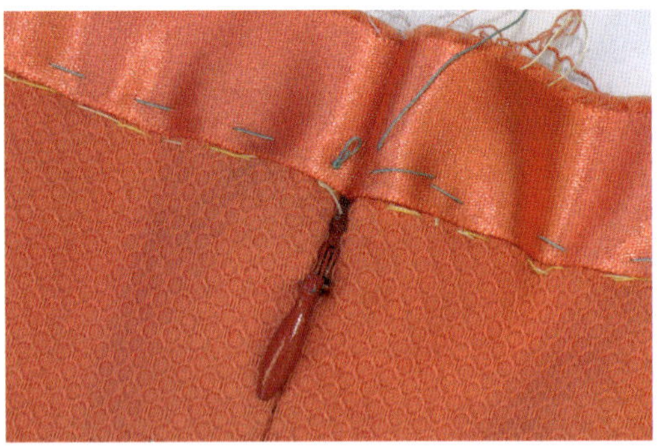

Figure 11.24

Add the facing

1. On the outside, place the wrong side of the ribbon on the dress seam allowance, resting the lower edge on the seamline, and baste in place. Before stitching the facing on permanently, it is a good idea to fasten the corselette and dress to check that all edges align at the centre back (Figure 11.24).

Figure 11.25

2. Adjust, if necessary, then edge stitch through all layers, catching the facing, the dress and the corselette. Trim and grade the seam allowances, then press them to the inside (Figure 11.25).

3. At the back edge, fold under the ribbon on the diagonal. Hand stitch it to the corselette along its length and at each end (Figure 11.26).

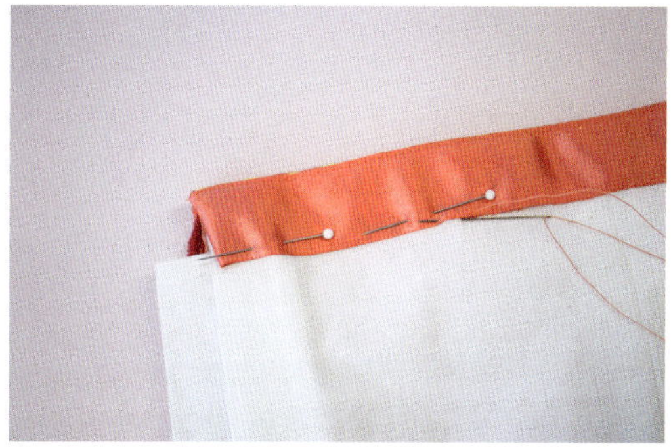

Figure 11.26

4. To prevent the corselette rolling to the outside, understitch the facing, securing it to the dress lining. Understitch about 1cm (⅜") below the upper edge, catching all layers except the outer one. Use a backstitch, and check that your stitching catches the lining but not the fashion fabric (Figure 11.27).

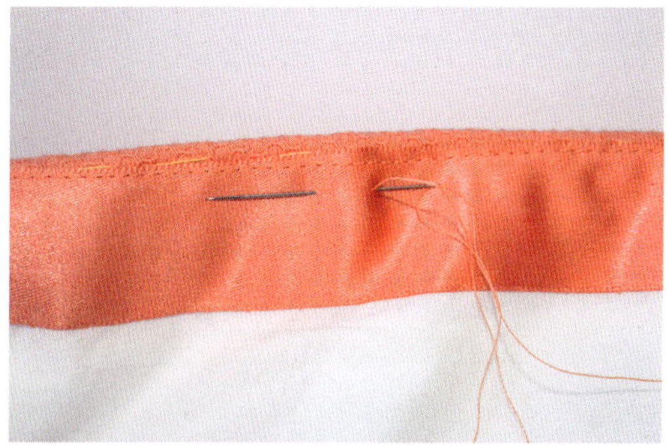

Figure 11.27

5. Lastly, sew a hook and eye on the facing above the zipper (Figure 11.28).

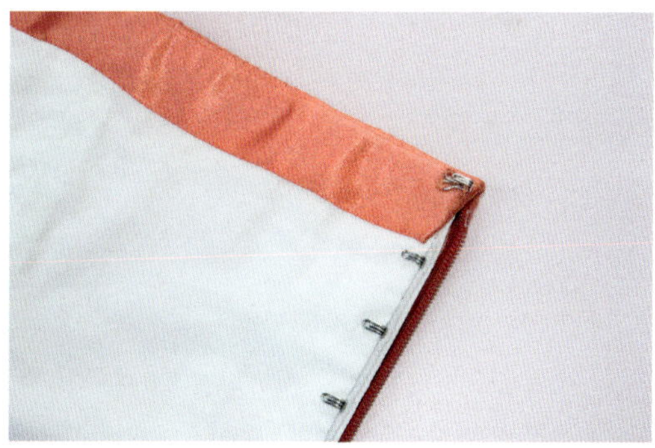

Figure 11.28

Hem the dress

Now the dress can be properly anchored on the body, allowing the hem to be marked. Try on the dress and measure the desired length. Finish by hemming the dress and lining.

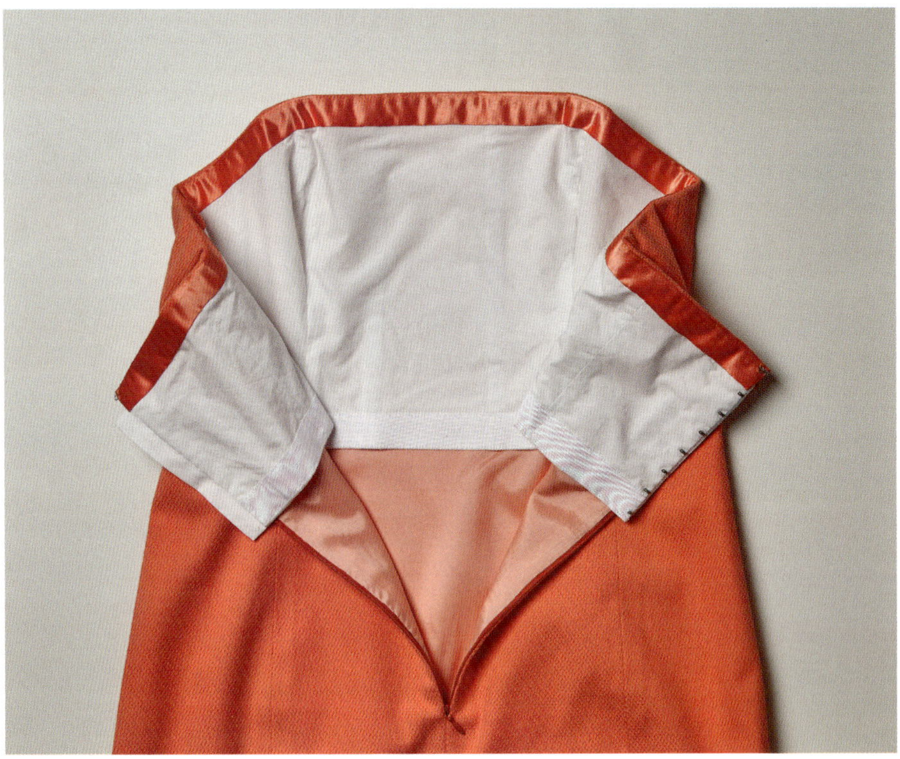

12

The Lace Wedding Gown

An elegant design of sequined lace and soft-flowing silk crêpe, this figure-hugging gown is romantic and sophisticated. A hip-length inner corselette anchors the gown firmly on the figure, smoothing the waist and abdomen to enhance the silhouette. The gown has a close fit with just a small amount of ease, while the corselette fit is even closer. This requires each to have its own fastening. The only common circumference is the upper edge, and this is where they'll be joined.

The inner corselette is a hip-length version of the gown, making it easy to develop the pattern. This allows us to focus on fit and other construction techniques. In this project we'll be working with cotton bobbinet and spiral steel boning, as well as applying a hand-sewn hook and eye closure. Although the bobbinet requires some special techniques to cut and prepare, it is quite easy to work with and the double-layer construction makes fitting adjustments easier.

Prepare the patterns

For this design we begin with a McCall's pattern for a strapless, princess-seamed evening gown. Although the pattern doesn't use an inner corselette, it is simple to develop from the gown pattern.

Prepare the gown pattern

Trace the panels for the gown and make any preliminary adjustments (such as cup size or bodice length). The crêpe and the lining can be cut on a double layer of fabric. The lace is best cut in a single layer so a complete set of pattern pieces should be prepared.

Create the corselette pattern

Trace the adjusted panels for the gown from the upper edge to about 12.5cm (5") below the waist. Add a seam and a dart at the centre front if you wish (Figure 12.1). As the corselette is developed from the gown pattern, it will have ease that isn't needed, especially at the waist and hips. During the toile fitting the ease is removed, the fit refined and the finished length determined.

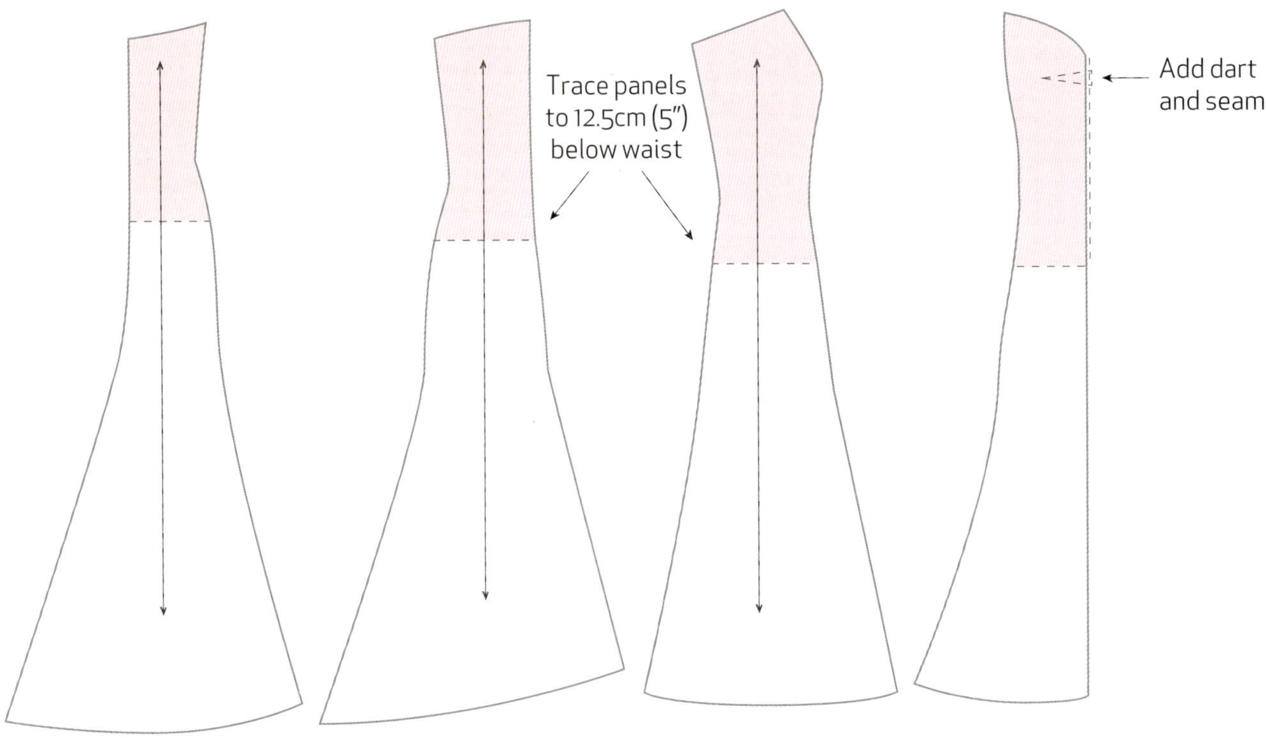

Figure 12.1

Sew and fit the toiles

Prepare toiles for both the inner corselette and the gown, basting boning in place on the corselette for the fitting. First fit both toiles separately, then fit them together. The two toiles must match at the upper edge, but below this the dress has a small amount of ease.

Fit the corselette toile

Make any length adjustments first, then increase or decrease the circumference in small amounts as needed, adjusting the toile to fit the figure snugly. Taking large amounts of fabric out from one place makes an exaggerated curve that never sits smoothly. If a large amount needs to be removed, adding narrow waist darts in the side front and side back panels to further snug in the waistline is better than taking all the excess from the seams.

Use the fitting to also check the depth and position of the centre front dart and mark the lower edge of the corselette. Assess where boning can best be placed to smooth the corselette and support the figure. Extra boning can be added over the dart locations, on the side front and side back panels, and at centre back to offer more support (Figure 12.2). The corselette and the gown will be joined along the upper edge, so any alterations made to the corselette upper edge need to be duplicated on the gown.

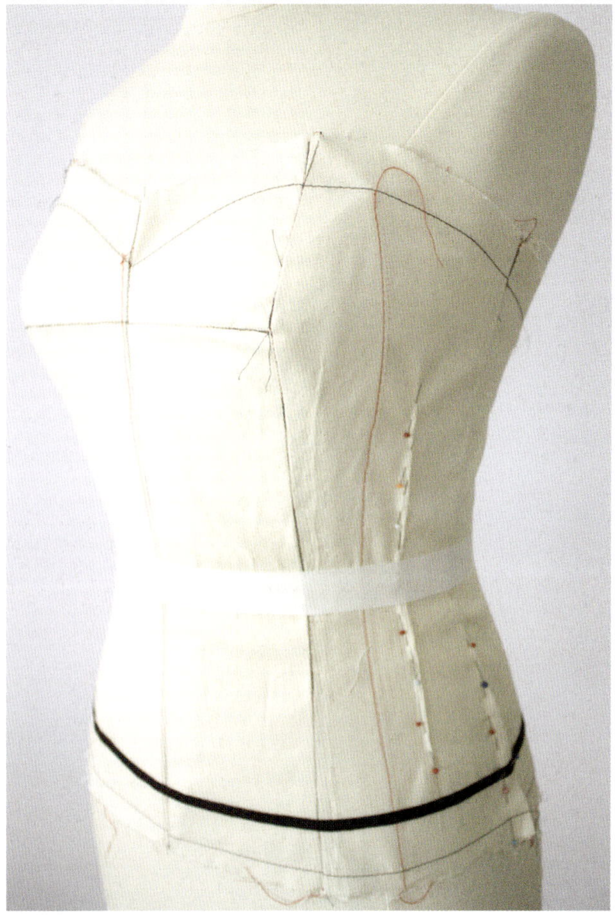

Figure 12.2

Fit the gown toile

First fit the gown toile separately, then fit it over the corselette toile, pinning them together at the upper edge. Establish the desired fit and length of the gown. The gown has a little more ease than the corselette so it gracefully skims the body rather than hugging it.

Figure 12.3

Construct the inner corselette

The lightweight corselette is created from two layers of cotton bobbinet cut on opposite grains to provide extra stability. It contains thirteen spiral steel bones in cotton tape casings and fastens with eleven hand-sewn hooks and eyes. Petersham ribbon is used for the waist stay. Cotton tape provides reinforcement for the hooks and eyes, which are covered with a facing (Figure 12.3).

Sew the corselette shell

Follow the process to construct a double-layer bobbinet corselette shell (see 'Assembling a double-layer bobbinet corselette', page 55). Cut the panels with wide seam allowances and thread trace the stitching lines (Figure 12.4). Join the panels, then finish the raw edges using a technique such as hand overcasting (Figure 12.5).

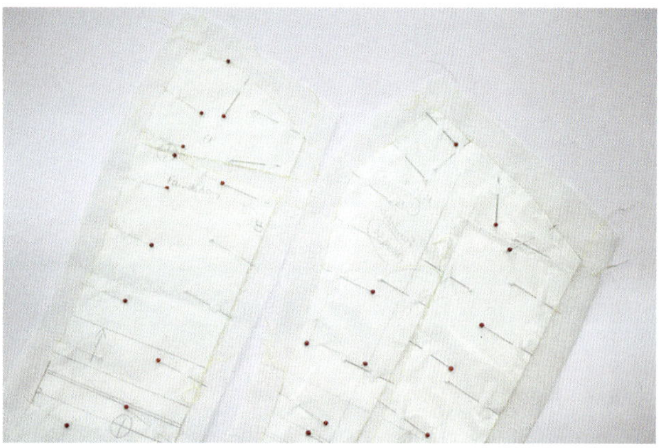

Figure 12.4

Figure 12.5

Add the bone casings

For this design, we will fold the bone casings under to keep them out of the upper seam allowance (Figure 12.6). Bones are placed on each seamline and over each vertical dart. In addition, bones are hidden behind the closure once it's completed, to better support the weight of the fabric at the centre back. Centre cotton tape over each seam and bone placement line, folding it under at the top edge and setting it back 3mm–6mm (⅛"–¼") from the upper seamline. Stitch in place, leaving the lower edge open (Figure 12.7).

Figure 12.6

Figure 12.7

Prepare the boning

Cut spiral steel boning to fit each casing and finish the ends with metal end caps (Figure 12.8). Check that they fit snugly in the casings then set them aside until needed.

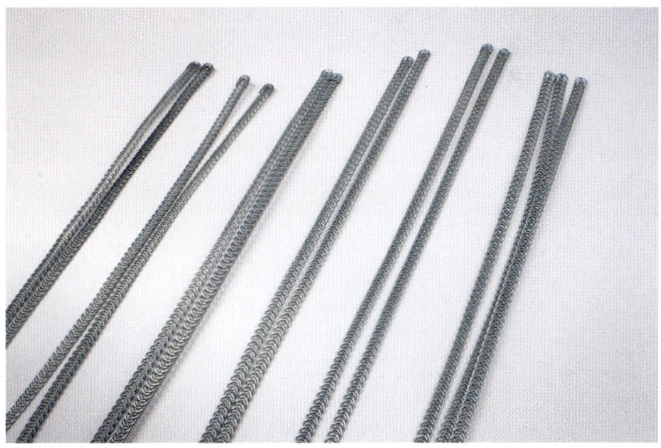

Figure 12.8

Figure 12.9

Stabilize the upper edge

Staystitch the upper edge, catching in a stay centred over the seamline (silk organza was used here) (Figure 12.9).

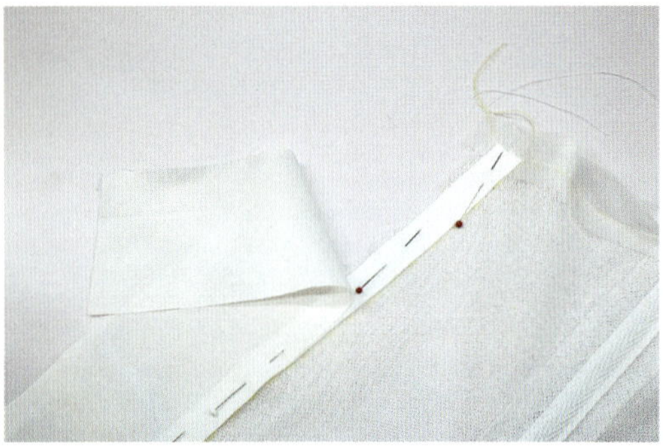

Figure 12.10

Add the closure

The back opening is reinforced with 12mm-wide (½"-wide) cotton tape. It incorporates a dupion facing to conceal the hardware and an extension to protect the wearer from the hooks. Channels are created behind the hooks and eyes to house additional boning.

1. Cut two lengths of cotton tape to fit the opening and place them on the seam allowances, aligning them with the seamline. Set the top edge of the tape just below the upper stitching line. Cut 5cm-wide (2"-wide) strips of dupion to fit the length of the opening and place over the tape. Baste through all layers then turn the seam allowance to the inside (Figure 12.10).
2. Stitch 3mm (⅛") from each edge and again 1cm (⅜") away. This secures the tape and creates a boning channel.
3. Sew hooks to the right back, stitching through the tape only, placing the top hook 2cm (¾") from the upper edge and set back 3mm (⅛") from the centre back. Sew the eyes to the left back, aligning them with the hooks and allowing a 3mm (⅛") overhang (Figure 12.11).

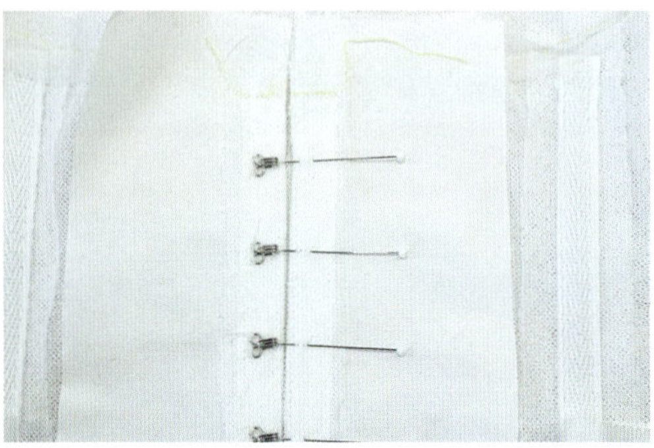

Figure 12.11

TIP

To keep from stitching through to the outside, place the boning in the channels before sewing the hooks and eyes.

Finish the facing

1. Prepare the extension by cutting a strip of dupion 6cm (2⅜") wide and the length of the opening. Fold it in half lengthwise and finish the upper edge. Baste the long edges together. Place the extension behind the eyes, setting it 1cm (⅜") below the upper edge. Baste it to the seam allowance (Figure 12.12).
2. Slipstitch it to the front edge between the eyes (Figure 12.13).
3. Fold under the facing edge and align the fold with the centre back. Slipstitch it to the extension (Figure 12.14).
4. On the right side, fold in the facing edge (Figure 12.15).

Figure 12.12

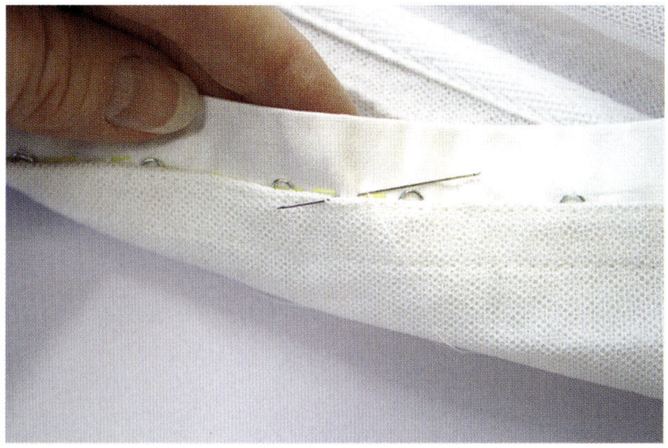

Figure 12.13

Figure 12.14

Figure 12.15

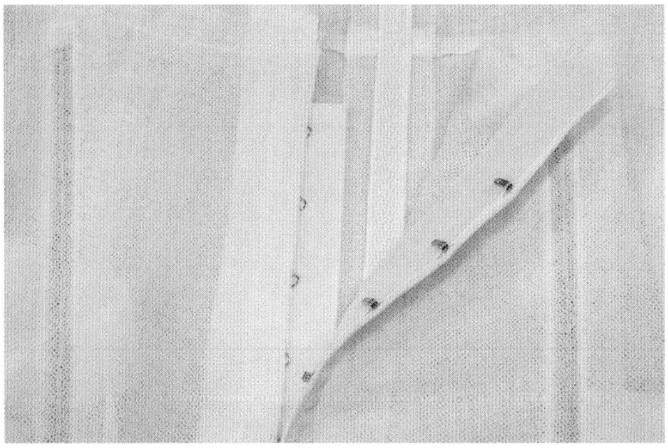

Figure 12.16

5. Slip it under the hooks then hand sew in place (Figure 12.16).

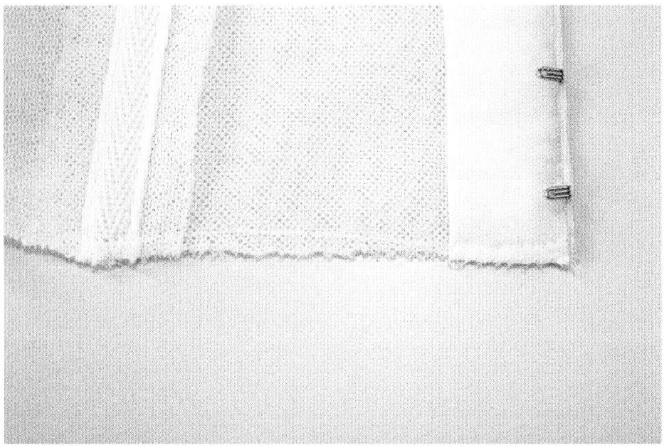

Figure 12.17

Install the boning and finish the edges

1. Insert the boning into the casings then stitch 6mm (¼") above the lower edge, securing it in place. Trim and hand overcast the raw edge (Figure 12.17).

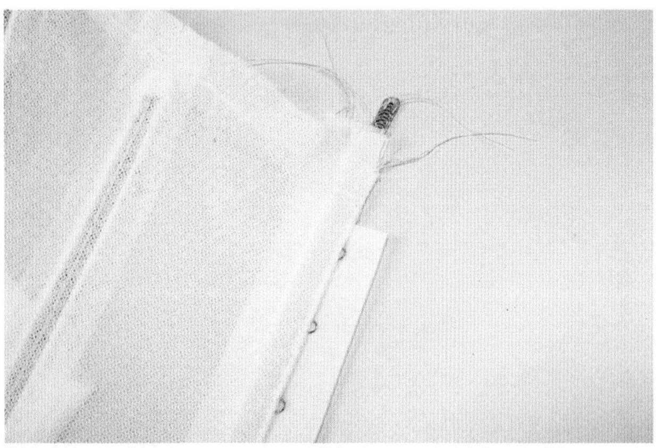

Figure 12.18

2. From the upper edge, insert the boning into the centre back channels, between the cotton tape and the facing. Baste across the facing at the upper edge on the seamline (Figure 12.18).

Attach the waist stay

Prepare the waist stay. Align the lower edge of the stay with the waist placement line and secure it at each bone casing (Figure 12.19). To finish, attach hanging loops to the upper edge (Figure 12.20).

Figure 12.19

Sew the gown

To achieve the desired silhouette, 4-ply silk crêpe was chosen for the gown, a fabric that is substantial enough for the close fit through the bust and torso, while having a nice drape in the skirt. A lightly sequinned lace is applied over the crêpe, adding some sparkle without weighing down the design. The lace is sewn into the seams with the crêpe through the torso, but falls separately through the lower skirt section.

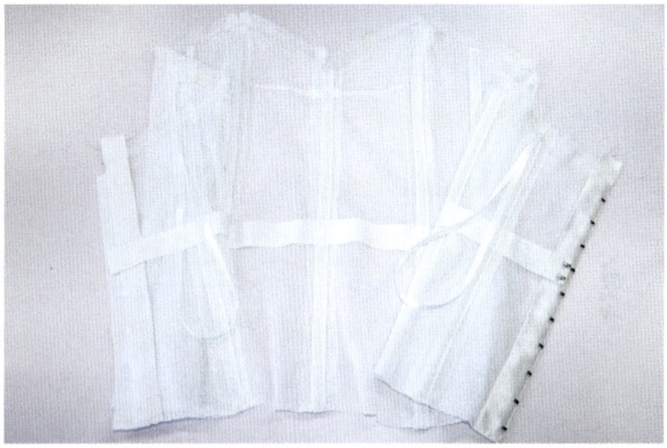

Figure 12.20

Cut and baste the layers

Cut two sets of pattern pieces: one from silk crêpe and one from lace. Reinforce each lace panel with staystitching at the point where the skirt flare begins and clip it at this point, allowing the lower section to be sewn separately. Layer each lace section on its corresponding crêpe piece and baste them together across the upper edge and along each seamline to the top of the flare (Figure 12.21). Next, baste the panels together from the upper edge to the top of the flare. Prior to sewing the panels, it's helpful to check the fit with the corselette basted in place, making any necessary changes.

Figure 12.21

Join the panels

The lower sections of the lace panels are finished first, as they are not joined to the crêpe. Sew the lace from the hem to the top of the flare, keeping the rest of the gown free. In this lace, a double seam trimmed close to the second row of stitching gave the best result, and was barely detectable. To finish joining the lower panels of the gown, pivot the lace out of the seam at the clip point and continue basting the seam in the crêpe only to the hem. Beginning at the lower edge, sew the panel seams, ensuring a smooth transition

Figure 12.22

where the lace joins into the seam (Figure 12.22). Press the gown seams open and the lower lace seams to one side. As the gown is not secured to the lining at the hem, finish the seam allowances to prevent them unravelling.

Stabilize and shape the upper edge

Staystitch the upper edge and apply cotton tape just above the stitching line. Ease the upper edge slightly onto the tape, cupping it into the body over the bust area (Figure 12.23).

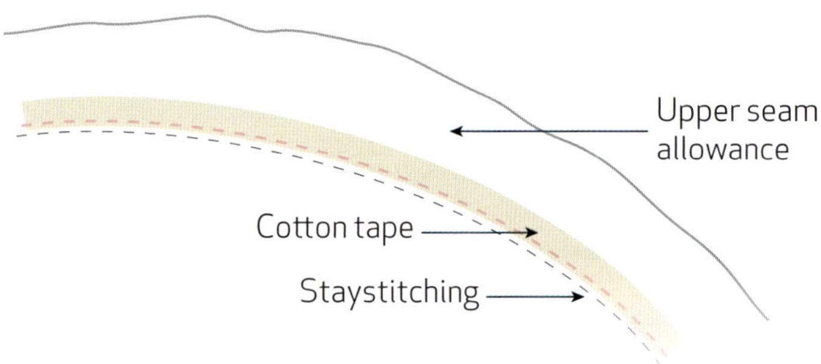

Figure 12.23

Figure 12.24

Add the zipper

Sew in a regular zipper in a centred application. Hand sewing is the best option when installing a zipper into lace. Set the top of the zipper 1cm (⅜") below the upper edge to allow space for a hook and eye and prevent it stacking on the corselette fastening (Figure 12.24).

Prepare and join the lining

Cut and sew the lining panels and finish the seam allowances. Slip the lining inside the gown, wrong sides together, matching the seamlines at the upper edge, and baste them together (Figure 12.25). Turn in the lining seam allowance at the back and slipstitch it to the zipper tape (Figure 12.26).

Figure 12.25

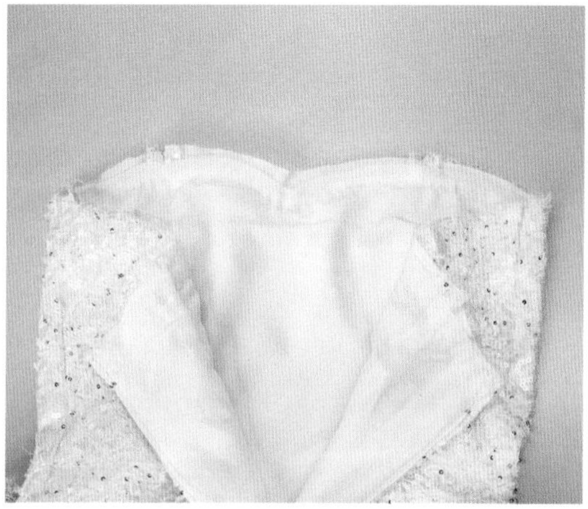

Figure 12.26

Join the inner corselette and gown

At this point, the corselette and the gown are finished and ready to be joined. Once this is completed, the gown can be hemmed. It is best to set the hem last, to ensure that the gown is properly anchored in place by the corselette.

Attach the corselette

Slip the corselette into the lined gown, with the right side of the corselette facing the lining, matching the seamlines at the upper edge. Baste the layers along the stitching line and secure the hanging loops (Figure 12.27).

Figure 12.27

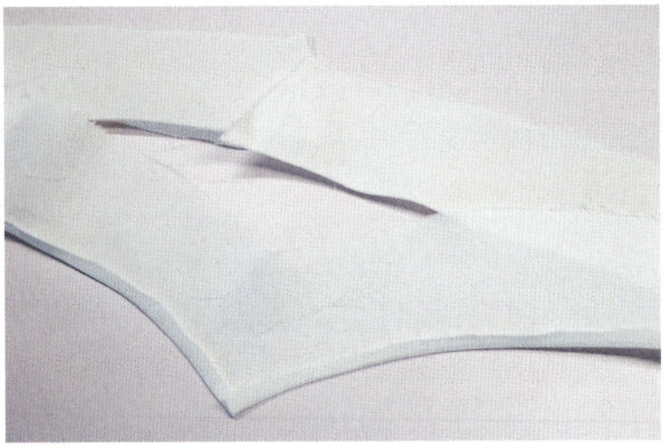

Figure 12.28

Add the facing

Prepare the facing, applying a light interfacing. Press the seams open then turn up and press the lower edge (Figure 12.28). With right sides together, sew the facing to the upper edge of the gown. Trim and clip the seam allowance. Turn the facing to the inside and understitch, keeping the gown and the corselette free.

Figure 12.29

Finish the upper edge

Fold the facing under on the diagonal at the back opening. Slip-stitch the facing to the corselette at the centre back and lower edge. To prevent the corselette rolling out, prick stitch through all layers except the lace 1cm (⅜") from the upper edge (Figure 12.29). Lastly, attach a hook and eye above the zipper.

Figure 12.30

Hem the skirt

Try on the gown and mark the hemline. Finish the crêpe and lining with narrow hems and apply an edging lace to the lace fabric. Connect the lace and crêpe with a French tack near the hemline at each seam (Figure 12.30).

Making a French tack (thread chain)

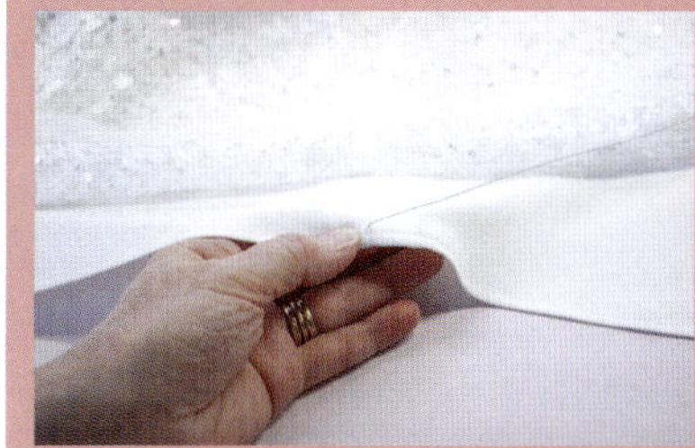

Step 1

Take a double strand of waxed thread and knot the end. Thread it through the fabric and anchor it with a small stitch on top.

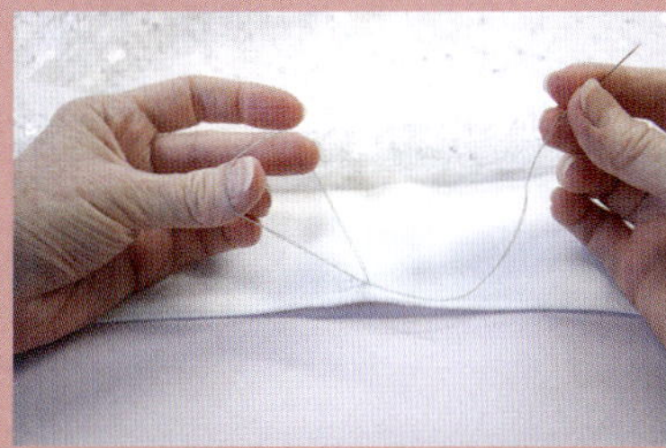

Step 2

Make a small backstitch in the same place, but do not pull the thread through completely. Leave a loop and a tail.

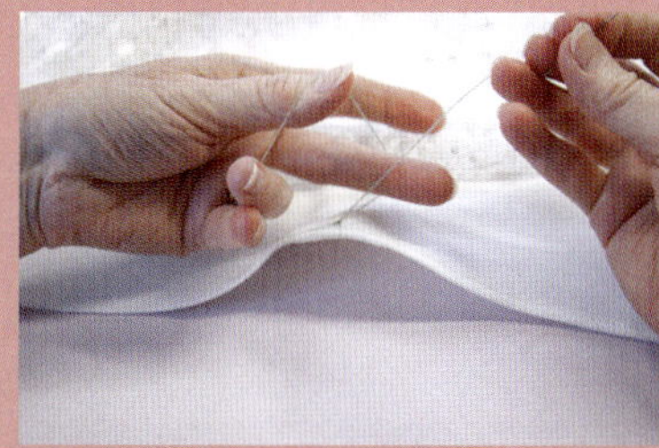

Step 3

Holding the loop open, pull the tail through the loop, making another loop.

Step 4

Pull the loop and tail, sliding it down to make a knot. Continue making loops to form a chain.

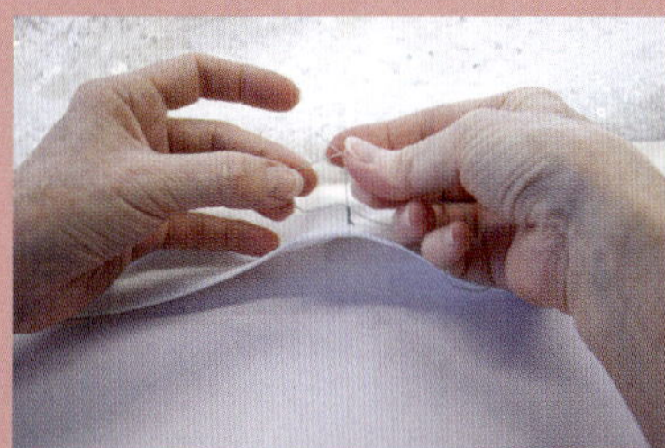

Step 5

When the chain is long enough, thread the needle through the last loop and pull tight to secure the chain.

Step 6

Insert the needle into the lace and secure the chain with a couple of stitches.

13

The Sweetheart Bare-Shouldered Jacket

Highlighting the decolletage and shoulders, this vibrant jacket is an elegant take on the classic tailored favourite. Perfect for pairing with cigarette pants or a pencil skirt, this design illustrates that inner corselettes are not just for dresses and gowns. The close-fitting jacket incorporates an inner corselette, a waist stay and elastic stays at the tops of the sleeves to keep everything secured.

A main focus for this project is working with sleeves, as they naturally require different considerations for support. Creating the patterns for this design is straightforward and we'll see how both are developed from an off-the-shoulder dress. This project uses a hip-length corselette, but, because of the loose fit of the jacket below the waist, a waist-length corselette would work as well. The bones are housed in channels rather than casings, a method that gives a neat, clean finish; however, alterations to the fit are difficult, so be confident with your toile fit before you begin. Plastic bones are used, and we'll look at the process of placing the corselette closure in the front. The corselette and the jacket are joined along the upper edge, with all seam allowances neatly hidden behind the lining.

Prepare the patterns

The starting point for this project is a Vogue pattern for an off-the-shoulder dress with princess seams, a fitted bodice and a straight or flared skirt. The design is easily adapted for both the corselette and the jacket patterns.

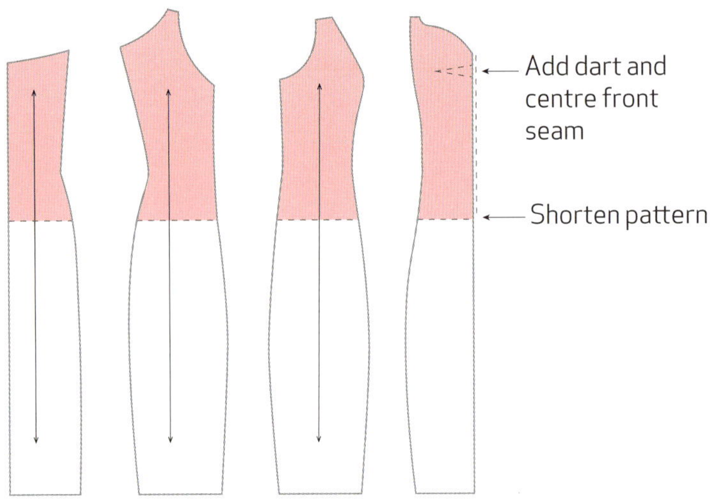

Figure 13.1

Create the corselette pattern

The pattern pieces for the straight skirt version of the dress form the basis for the corselette pattern. Place a seam at the centre front for the closure, adding a dart if desired. The sleeve pattern won't be used and the skirt is shortened to 15cm (6") below the waist (Figure 13.1).

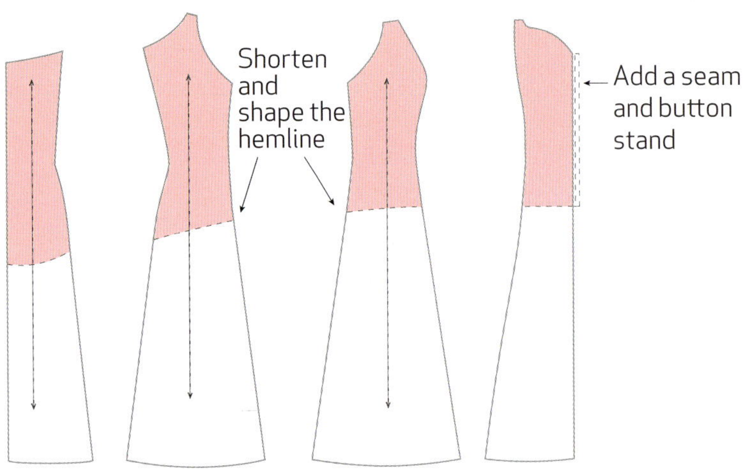

Figure 13.2

Create the jacket pattern

The jacket pattern was created from the view with the flared skirt (the upper section of the two designs are the same). A seam was added at the centre front for the closure and a button stand placed on the left front. The skirt was shortened to hip length and reshaped for a high-low look, and the sleeve length adjusted to complement the jacket length (Figure 13.2).

Sew and fit the toiles

Create a toile each for the jacket and the corselette, basting boning to the corselette panels. Place additional boning on the front and back side panels, ending near the top of the armhole. This is important in an off-the-shoulder design as it's the high point of the bodice and needs support (Figure 13.3).

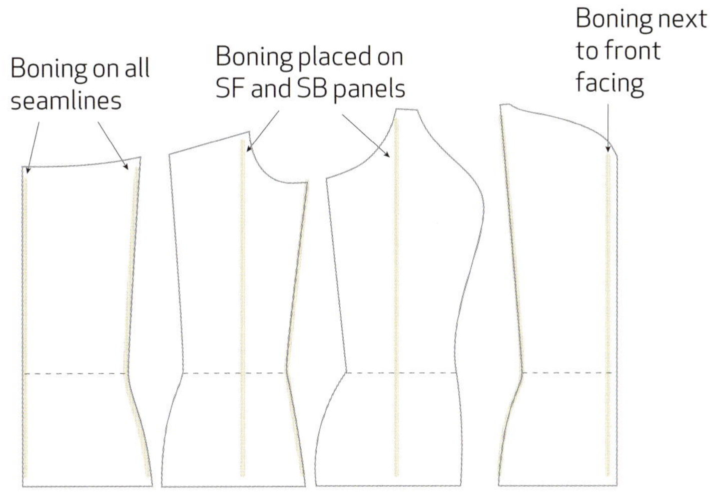

Figure 13.3

First fit the corselette, making it snug through the torso (Figure 13.4). The corselette supports the jacket from the waist, not the upper edge, so it's unnecessary to make the upper edge too tight. Allow it to sit comfortably next to the body. Mark the positions of the waistline and the lower edge. Remember to copy any changes to the corselette upper edge onto the jacket pattern as well, so that the two will match for joining.

Next, the jacket toile is fitted, adjusting the bodice to get the desired fit. As mentioned, the upper edges need to match, but, below that, the jacket has a small amount of ease to the waist where it then flares out. Review the fit of the armhole, which should be close-fitting but comfortable. Having the upper edge of the sleeve slightly away from the shoulder and a close-fitting armhole (about 2.5cm (1") below the armpit) will allow for more movement. Off-the-shoulder garments with fitted sleeves are notoriously hard to move in, and getting this balance right will help. Finally, pin the two toiles together for a check fit.

Figure 13.4

Figure 13.5

Construct the inner corselette

The corselette is constructed from a double layer of cotton, cut on opposite grains. It's supported by thirteen covered plastic bones installed in channels (rather than their casings); it closes with hook and eye tape at the centre front; and it is secured in place with a Petersham ribbon waist stay. The construction is neatly hidden and the corselette joins the jacket along the upper edge, but remains free at the armhole where it is finished with binding (Figure 13.5).

Sew the corselette shell

Prepare the two layers for a lined corselette, placing the opening at the centre front (Figure 13.6). Press the seams open and clip as necessary. Place the two layers wrong sides together, carefully aligning each seamline. Baste along the seamlines through all layers, leaving the front edges free (Figure 13.7).

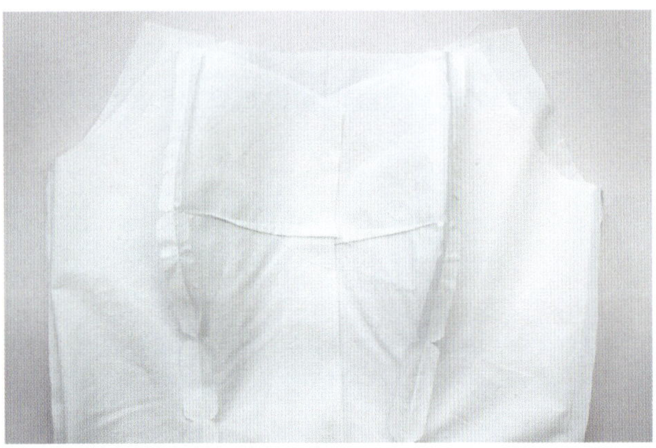

Figure 13.6

Figure 13.7

Sew the boning channels and prepare the boning

Form the boning channels by sewing two parallel rows of stitching along each seam and bone placement line, sewing from edge to edge. It is a good idea to make a sample to test the distance between rows to fit your boning width snugly (Figure 13.8). Measure the length of each boning channel between the upper and the lower stitching lines and cut boning to fit. Finish the ends and check their fit in the channels. Set the bones aside.

Figure 13.8

Apply the hook and eye tape

As the hooks face outwards in this design, the tape is attached to the lining first, then covered with the outer layer.

1. Place the hook tape on the right front (facing outwards) and the eyes on the left front. Stitch the tapes to the seam allowances then fold them to the inside (Figure 13.9).

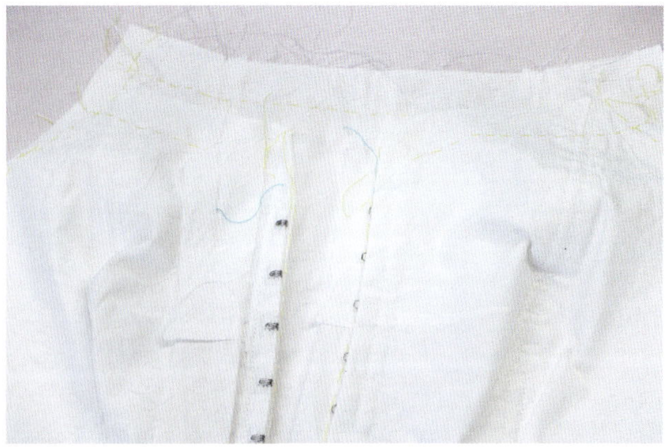

Figure 13.9

2. Turn under the remaining seam allowances, cover the tapes and slipstitch in place by hand along the outer edge (Figure 13.10). Staystitch along the upper edge.

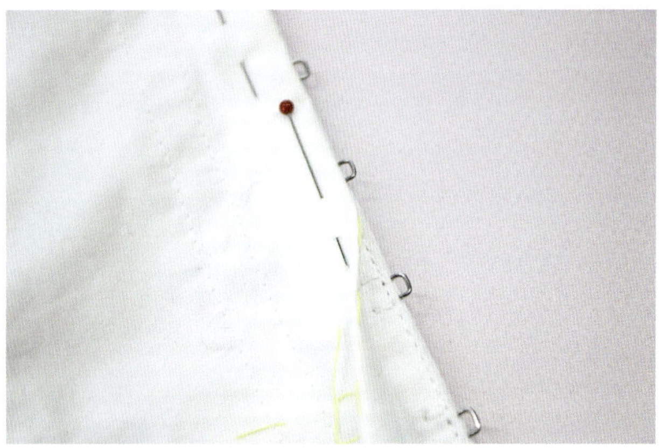

Figure 13.10

Figure 13.11

Bind the armhole

The armhole won't be attached to the jacket, so the edges need to be finished. Trim the seam allowance from the armhole edge then staystitch 6mm (¼") from the cut edge. Cut a 3cm-wide (1¼"-wide) bias strip of cotton and bind the edge (Figure 13.11).

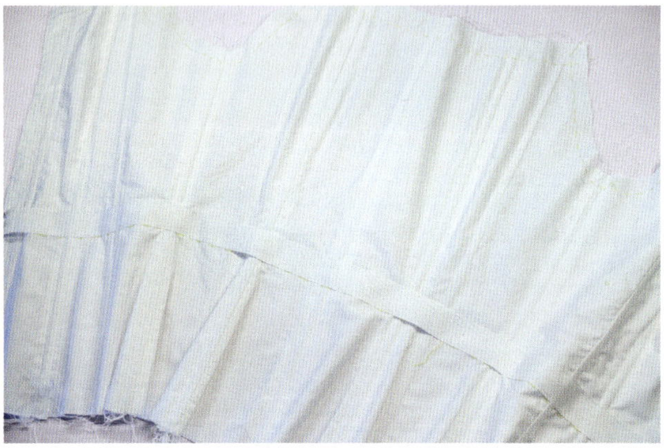

Figure 13.12

Prepare the waist stay

Create the waist stay to fit the waist measurement. Place the lower edge on the waistline and stitch it to the corselette by machine along both edges, breaking the stitching at each boning channel and leaving it free for 2.5cm (1") from centre front (Figure 13.12).

Sew the jacket

The cut of this jacket requires a fabric that holds its shape well, supporting the off-the-shoulder neckline as well as the peplum. Jacquard was chosen for the fashion fabric, and silk organza underlining provides additional lightweight support. Silk satin is used to both line the jacket and create the button loops. Other supplies needed to complete the jacket include cotton tape, elastic and horsehair trim for the sleeves and buttons for the closure.

Prepare and sew the panels

Underline each panel then baste the jacket together for a fitting over the corselette (Figure 13.13). Assess the fit of the two garments together and make any adjustments to the jacket that are needed. Importantly, check that the lengths match at the upper edge and that the sleeve sits a little away from the body. Sew the panels together then trim and press the seams open, clipping as necessary. Stitch the sleeve underarm seam, but do not join it to the bodice. When using a particularly springy fabric such as this jacquard, catchstitching the allowances to the underlining will keep them lying flat.

Figure 13.13

Stabilize and shape the upper edge

Staystitch the upper edge, then apply cotton stay tape to the front panels to stabilize the curved edge. Place the tape just above the stitching line, easing the upper edge slightly to cup it towards the body (Figure 13.14).

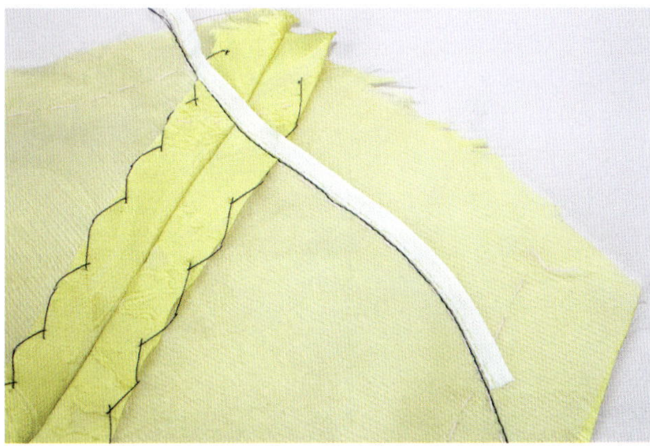

Figure 13.14

Sew the lining

Join the bodice lining panels together and staystitch the upper edge. Prepare the sleeve linings, but do not join them to the bodice yet.

Prepare the sleeves

Begin by stitching the lining and the sleeve at the upper edge, right sides together. Next, apply 2.5cm-wide (1"-wide) horsehair trim to the upper edge. This gives the upper edge of the sleeve extra support to keep it from collapsing. Cover the ends of the trim to prevent unravelling then stitch it to the seam allowance, extending each end into the armscye seam (Figure 13.15).

Turn the lining and trim to the inside and understitch, then catchstitch the lower edge of the trim to the underlining (Figure 13.16). Baste the layers together at the armscye and finish the hems. Set the sleeves aside until needed.

Figure 13.15

Figure 13.16

Construct the button loops

Create the rouleau button loops from bias strips of the silk satin lining. To make the loops uniform, it helps to first sew them to a paper template (Figure 13.17). Next, sew them to the right side of the jacket front along the seamline (Figure 13.18).

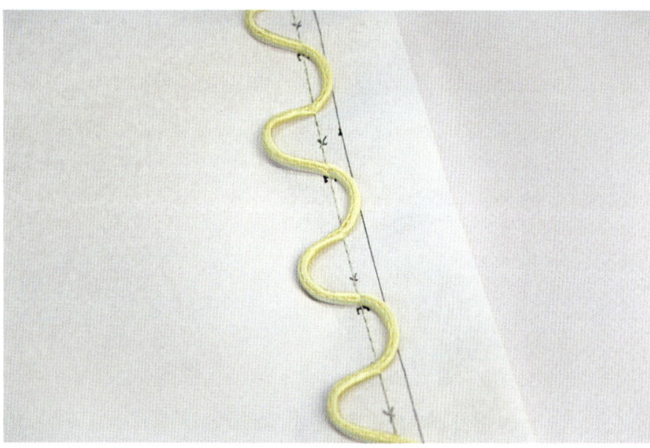

Figure 13.17

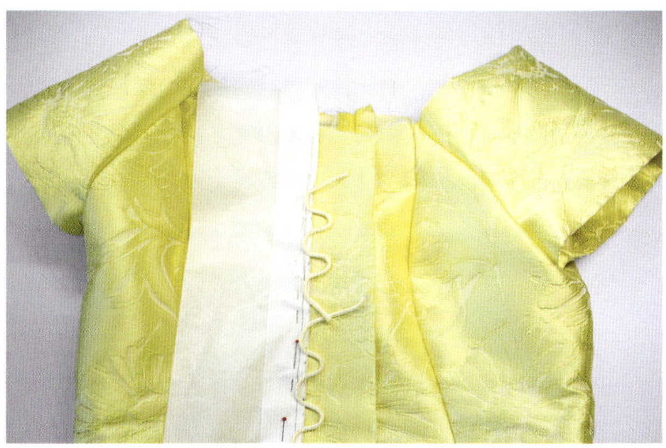

Figure 13.18

Join the inner corselette and jacket

With the jacket and corselette near completion, they are ready to be connected before applying the finishing elements. It's easier to remove the boning while joining the layers. In this design, the boning is easily added as one of the final steps.

Connect the layers

1. Place the wrong side of the corselette on the outside of the jacket, matching the upper seamlines of the front and back necklines, and baste them together (Figure 13.19).
2. Next, place the right side of the lining over the corselette, matching the seamlines along the upper edges as before, and baste through all layers (Figure 13.20).

Figure 13.19

Figure 13.20

3. Sew the upper edge, trim and clip the seam allowances then turn the corselette and lining to the inside. Fold the seam allowances towards the lining and corselette and understitch the upper edge (Figure 13.21).

Figure 13.21

Complete the jacket and corselette

With the corselette and jacket now joined, the final details can be completed. Attach the sleeves to the jacket, then the front edge can be finished and the hem sewn in place. The corselette boning is then re-inserted and the lower edge finished with a binding.

Attach the sleeves and finish the armholes

Figure 13.22

1. Keeping the corselette free, baste the lining and the jacket together at each armhole, matching the seamlines, then sew in the completed sleeves.
2. Cut a length of 1cm-wide (⅜"-wide) elastic as a stay, to snugly fit the top of each arm, plus seam allowances. Cover each stay with a casing of lining fabric cut long enough to allow the elastic to stretch. Baste one stay into each armscye, matching the seamlines. Try the jacket on to check that the elastic fits snugly around the upper arms, then secure the stays in place along the seamlines.
3. Trim the armscye seam allowances to 6mm (¼"). Attach hanging loops either side of each underarm seam, then bind the seam allowances with lining fabric (Figure 13.22).

Figure 13.23

Finish the front edge and hem the jacket

Join the jacket and the lining at the front edge. Turn up the jacket hem and stitch in place, then join the lining at the hemline. Understitch the front edges by hand and sew on the buttons (Figure 13.23).

Finish the corselette

Insert the boning into the channels then sew along the lower stitching line to secure the boning. Finish the lower edge with binding, using a 3cm-wide (1¼"-wide) bias strip of cotton (Figure 13.24).

Figure 13.24

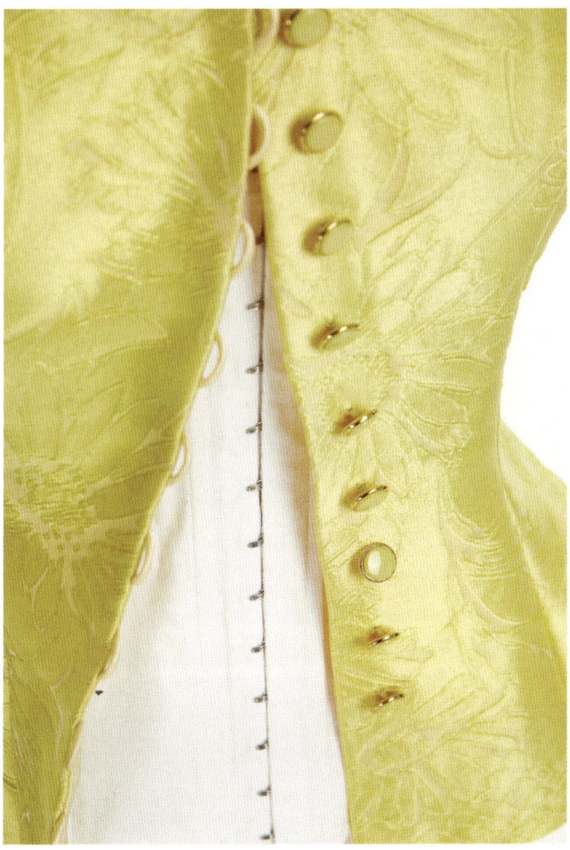

14

The Blush Tea-Length Gown

Capturing the feminine silhouette of the 1950s, this gown features a fitted bodice, a slim waist and a full skirt enhanced by a built-in underdress consisting of a corselette and a tulle petticoat. The gown and the underdress are completed as separate pieces, then joined by hand. This project uses several new techniques with a slightly higher level of difficulty. The corselette and the gown must match at several points (not just the upper edge) and the pattern is altered to create the outer design.

Here we'll explore how to adapt a strapless, princess-seamed sheath to create both the corselette and the gown patterns. The construction of the lined corselette with plastic boning and casings will be familiar; however, this project also shows the steps involved in attaching the petticoat, the different methods of fastening the corselette and petticoat and how to hand sew the corselette into the gown. Once the two are joined securely by hand, the underdress eliminates the need for the gown to be lined separately.

Prepare the patterns

The patterns for both the corselette and the gown are developed using a Vogue evening design: a close-fitting strapless gown with princess seams and a sweetheart neckline. A classic style like this is ideal for creating a unique gown with an inner corselette. Developing both the gown and the corselette patterns from the same pattern ensures that they will match in all key areas and some simple modifications to the original pattern will allow a new design to be developed.

In this design, it is essential that the two patterns match precisely where they will be connected: the upper edge and the empire seam. For example, if a centre front dart is used in the corselette, cupping it into the bust, the dart volume also needs to be included in the gown so that they fit together at centre front. The dart can be stitched, folded out or converted to a pleat or gathers in the gown, or it could be left out of both garments. In this project the dart is included in both, stitching it in the corselette and folding it out of the dress pattern.

Create the corselette pattern

Preparing the hip-length corselette pattern is simple, as it is a shortened version of the evening gown. Trace the gown panels from the upper edge to the hip onto tissue paper then lower the upper edge 1cm (⅜"), setting it below the gown upper edge. A centre front seam was added and a dart was placed at bust level to pull the corselette into the sternum. Add a 1.5cm (⅝") hem allowance at the upper edge and mark a stitching line 6mm (¼") above the lower edge where the boning will end (Figure 14.1).

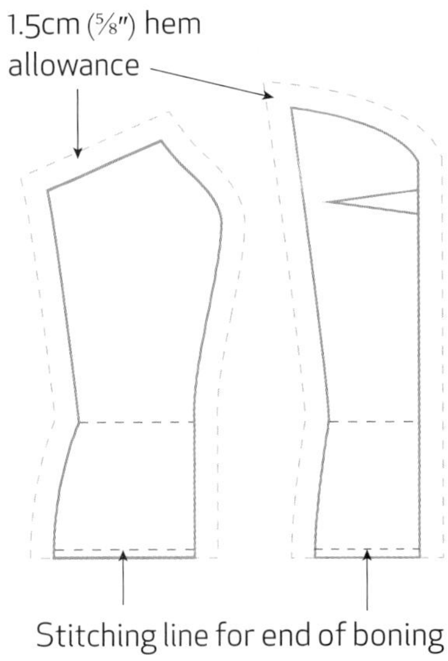

Figure 14.1

Adapt the pattern for the gown design

Trace the panels again to the desired length for the gown, adding the centre front seam and marking the bust dart. Flare each panel below the waist to create the desired amount of fullness in the skirt (Figure 14.2). Prepare the bodice by folding out the centre front dart, then true the seam (Figure 14.3).

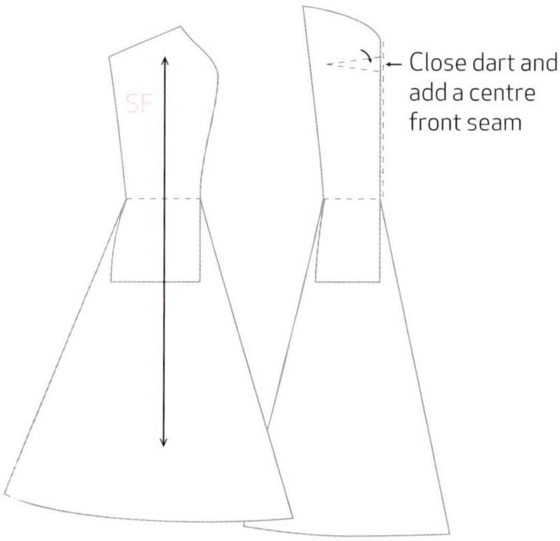

Figure 14.2

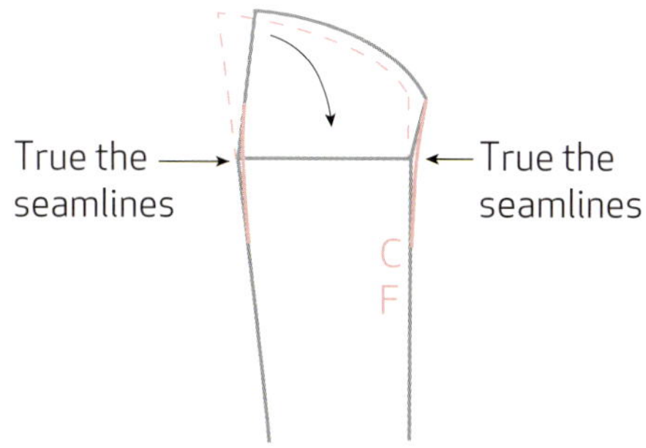

Figure 14.3

As the front upper edge is quite curved, a separate facing will work best here, giving a smoother fit. Draft the front facing then mark a placement line for the corselette 1cm (⅜") below the upper edge on both the front and the back facing (Figure 14.4).

Add a 4cm (1½") extended facing to the back upper edge. Mark the corselette placement line on the facing side of the upper edge. Once the facing is turned inwards, the placement line will then be positioned below the upper edge. The empire seam is not marked on the pattern at this point, allowing for its position to be experimented with during the toile fitting.

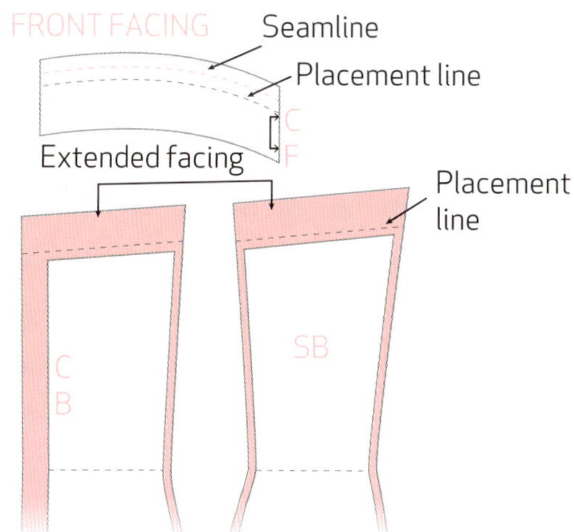

Figure 14.4

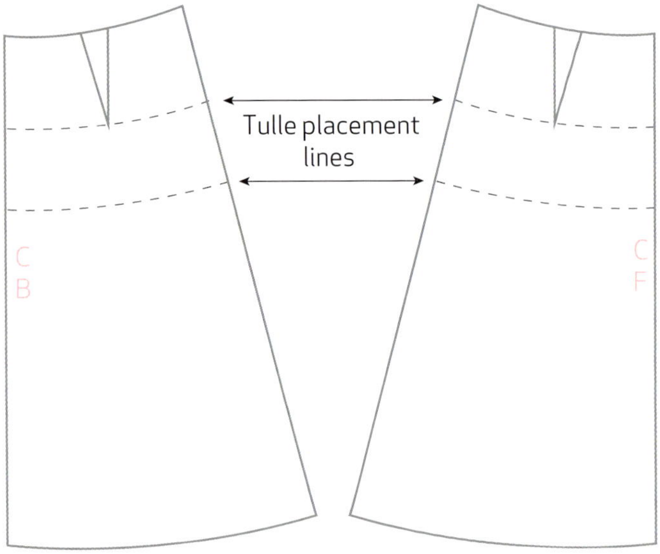

Figure 14.5

Prepare the petticoat pattern

The petticoat is a basic A-line skirt pattern from Vogue. The waist measurement matches that of the corselette waist but there is ease at the hips. Two placement lines for the tulle ruffles were marked on the petticoat 8cm (3⅛") and 20cm (8") below the waist (Figure 14.5).

Figure 14.6

Sew and fit the toiles

Prepare toiles for both the corselette and the gown. The corselette and the gown have the same fit from the upper edge to the empire seam and any changes in this area must be duplicated on both toiles. Below this point, the corselette is snug while the gown has ease. Check that the petticoat waist matches the corselette waist and prepare a toile if you would like to check the overall fit.

Fine-tune the fit of the corselette

Adjust the toile so that it is snug, determine the length and mark the waistline. Check the depth and position of the bust dart and whether boning placement is adequate. Mark the end of the bones 6mm (¼") above the lower edge (Figure 14.6).

Fit the gown toile

Adjust the fit of the upper bodice to match any changes made to the corselette. This is the time to experiment with the position of the empire seam, marking out options with cotton tape (Figure 14.7). The final position of the seam is transferred to both the gown and the corselette patterns. With all changes made, the gown toile is fitted over the corselette toile, pinning the corselette upper edge 1cm (⅜") below the gown upper edge where it will be later joined. Make a final check to ensure that the fit is correct and the match points correspond.

Figure 14.7

Construct the inner corselette and petticoat

In this design, the corselette and the petticoat also function as the lining. Silk taffeta is a great choice for their construction as the gown can move freely over the smooth base. The lined inner corselette is created from two layers on opposite grains. It is lightly boned, having seven pieces of synthetic whalebone in Petersham casings, one on each seamline. The taffeta petticoat has two layers of tulle ruffles (Figure 14.8). Other supplies required include a regular dress zipper, 1.5cm-wide (⅝"-wide) Petersham ribbon for the upper edge facing and 2.5cm-wide (1"-wide) Petersham ribbon for the waist stay. Seam binding and hooks and eyes are also needed to provide the finishing touches to the petticoat.

Figure 14.8

Figure 14.9

Sew the corselette shell

Create the two corselette layers following the process for a lined corselette. The seam allowances are pinked, as taffeta frays easily, and this helps protect the shells as they are worked on. Backstitch the centre front seam at the upper edge exactly where the two panels meet. Thread trace the upper edge, waistline and empire seam placement line on both layers then set the lining aside (Figure 14.9).

Figure 14.10

Add the bone casings and prepare the boning

To form casings on the outer layer, centre Petersham ribbon over each seam, running from edge to edge, and stitch in place. On the centre front seam, turn under the end of the casing and place the fold at bust level to finish the boning here (Figure 14.10). Cut lengths of synthetic whalebone to fit each casing and finish the ends, setting them aside until needed.

Figure 14.11

Join the layers and finish the upper edge

1. Baste the corselette and the lining wrong sides together, matching the placement lines and seam-lines (Figure 14.11). Attach hanging loops if desired.

2. Cut two lengths of 1.5cm-wide (⅝"-wide) Petersham ribbon to fit the upper edge from centre front to centre back and shape them with steam to match the curve (Figure 14.12).
3. Fold in the upper edge of the corselette on the foldline and cover with the ribbon, lapping them at centre front. Edgestitch through all layers then hand stitch the lower edge to the corselette lining (Figure 14.13).

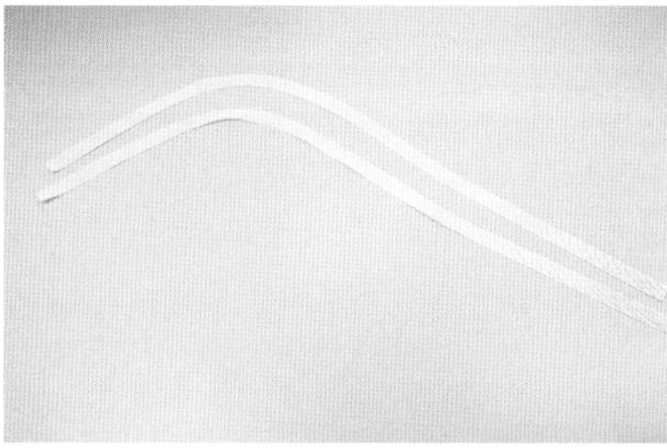

Figure 14.12

Figure 14.13

Install the boning and finish the lower edge

Place the boning into the casings and machine stitch the lower edges together. Finish the raw edge with hand overcasting (Figure 14.14).

Figure 14.14

Install the zipper

Finish the centre back seam allowances. Sew in the zipper by machine using a centred application, leaving the extra length below the corselette hemline. Set the zipper 1cm (⅜") below the upper edge and sew a hook and eye above it (Figure 14.15).

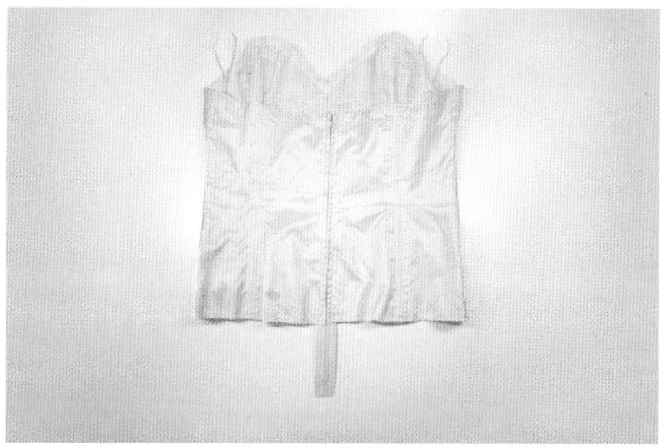

Figure 14.15

Create and attach the petticoat

Figure 14.16

1. Staystitch the waistline and mark the tulle placement lines on the petticoat, then sew the seams, leaving an opening in the centre back from waist to hip (Figure 14.16). Turn in the opening seam allowances and secure. Cut pieces of tulle that are three times (or as desired) the length of each placement line, reaching to the hemline. Gather the top edges and sew the centre back seams to match the petticoat opening depth, folding the opening edges to the inside.

Figure 14.17

2. Pin the lower ruffle to the petticoat, adjusting the gathers. Stitch, then cover the seam allowance with seam binding. Attach the upper ruffle in the same way then sew a hook and eye at the end of each row of tulle so that the back edges meet when closed (Figure 14.17).

Figure 14.18

3. Turn in the petticoat waist seam, clipping as needed. Pin to the corselette, matching the waistline and centre back. Slipstitch the petticoat to the corselette at the waist (Figure 14.18).

Add the waist stay

Prepare the waist stay. Place the lower edge of the stay on the waistline and stitch to the corselette at each seam, and 2.5cm (1") either side of the zipper (Figure 14.19).

Figure 14.19

Sew the gown

The main fabric used to construct the gown is jacquard, a lightweight fabric with body, which makes it perfect for both the structured bodice and the full skirt. A silk organza underlining supports the skirt's volume, which is further enhanced by the ruffled petticoat attached to the corselette. Taffeta underlines the bodice, giving it added support. Remember that any changes made to the fit of the corselette above the empire seam need to be transferred to the gown pattern so that they will match. To begin, underline the gown and baste it together for a fitting over the corselette.

Construct the lower gown

Sew the panels of the lower gown (Figure 14.20). For smoother seams, sew all the panels in the same direction, from the hem to the upper edge. Clip the seam allowances then press them open, using a curved surface through the waist area to build shape into the design.

Figure 14.20

Figure 14.21

As the gown won't be lined, the seam allowances need to be finished. Hand overcasting is a good choice as it is unobtrusive and doesn't stiffen the seams (Figure 14.21).

Prepare the bodice front

Join the front panels and staystitch the upper edge. Stabilize and shape the upper edge with cotton tape, easing it gently onto the tape over the bust (Figure 14.22). Prepare the front facing, taking care to mark both the upper stitching line (yellow) and the placement line for the corselette (blue) (Figure 14.23). Join the facing to the front bodice along the upper edge. Press the seam allowances towards the facing and understitch them.

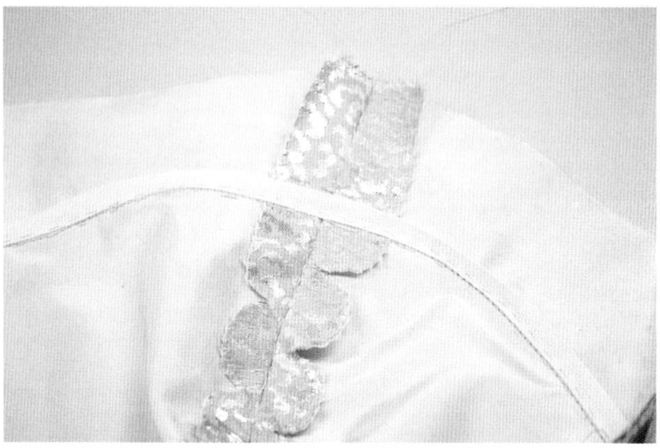

Figure 14.22

Figure 14.23

Finish the bodice and assemble the gown

Join the back panels and staystitch the upper edge on the foldline. Sew the front and back sections together at the sides, continuing up through the facings. Next, sew the bodice to the lower gown, matching the centres and seamlines. Hand overcast the seam allowances and press them towards the bodice. To achieve a smooth finish at the upper edge, mitre the join between the facing and the centre back, then hand overcast the seam allowances and catchstitch them to the underlining.

Add the fastening

Finish the gown by installing a centred zipper into the back opening. Set it 1cm (⅜") below the upper edge and place a hook and eye above it (Figure 14.24).

Figure 14.24

Join the inner corselette and gown

Now that the corselette and the gown are complete, most of the hard work is done. All that remains is for the two to be joined at the empire seam and the upper edge.

Connect the layers

1. Slip the gown over the underdress. Match the empire seam with the placement line on the corselette. Pin together and sew invisibly along the gown seam through all layers, leaving 2.5cm (1") free each side of the zipper (Figure 14.25).

Figure 14.25

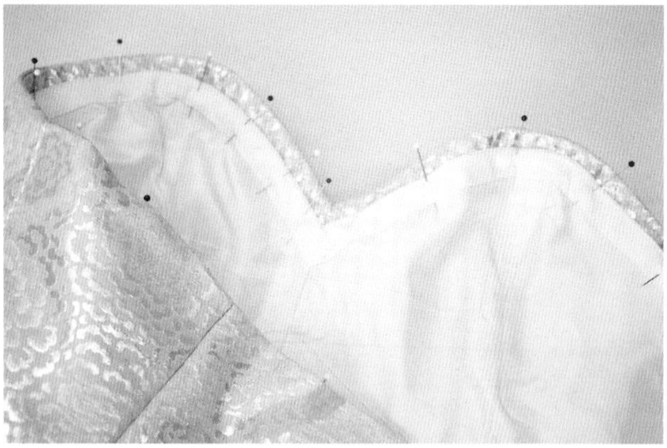

Figure 14.26

2. Smooth the upper bodice over the corselette, matching them at the side seams and the princess seams. Pin the corselette on the placement line 1cm (⅜") below the gown upper edge then slipstitch it to the gown facing and underlining, stopping 2.5cm (1") either side of centre back (Figure 14.26).

Figure 14.27

Finish the hems

Try on the gown and measure the desired length. Finish the gown hem with a 10cm (4") deep facing. Cover the raw edge with seam binding and slipstitch it to the underlining (Figure 14.27). Mark the petticoat hemline 2.5cm (1") shorter than the gown. Turn up a narrow hem (1cm or ⅜") and stitch in place. Trim the tulle if necessary, so that it is even and not visible.

15

The Floral Evening Gown

Cut in a delicate silk satin, this romantic silhouette features soft florals and an elegant floor-length full skirt, all supported by a hip-length corselette. Above the waist the gown and the corselette have the same fit, allowing the use of a single fastening for both, while below the waist the closer fit of the corselette smooths the figure under the circular skirt.

The main challenge of this project lies in developing the patterns from a princess seamed sheath rather than a strapless design. However, although it includes a few more steps, the process is not difficult. We'll look first at how to develop the strapless design, and then at how it is adapted to create the corselette and gown patterns. This project delves into how to make the bones less visible as well as the method of hand sewing the corselette into a bodice with an extended facing. As the corselette and the bodice have the same fit, there is a single fastening for both, while the skirt closes over the top of the corselette with a separate fastener. We'll go step-by-step through the process, achieving a garment that allows the skirt to float gracefully away from the body. As a final step, we'll also discuss how to make and then sew bust padding into your corselette.

Create and fit the strapless design

There are several extra steps involved to create the patterns for this gown and more than one toile will be needed to achieve a good fit. First is adapting a sheath dress to a strapless design with a close fit, from which the final patterns are then developed. Beginning with a Simplicity pattern for a day dress with princess seams to the shoulders, the final pattern is developed during the toile fittings. This is where the upper edge shape is determined, the waistline marked, the length and fit established and the bust dart draped.

Convert the pattern to a strapless design

Begin by choosing the pattern size, having finished measurements slightly larger than needed, as it is easier to remove fabric to shape the garment during the fitting than to add it. Trace the pattern from the shoulders to 15cm (6") below the waist and make preliminary adjustments for the figure. Lastly, add a centre front seam and increase the seam allowances to 2.5cm (1").

Construct and fit the toile

If bust padding will be used in the gown, baste it in place prior to the toile fitting. Pin the seams for a close fit and drape a dart at the centre front if desired. Decide on the upper edge design, mark the waistline and the lower edge, then transfer the alterations to the pattern for a second toile (Figure 15.1).

When there are many changes, making a second toile is essential in order to reassess the fit. In particular, focus on the neckline, which will need tightening once the shoulder area is removed. It is a good idea to baste boning in for the second fitting to determine its final positions. Repeat the fitting and then transfer all new changes to the pattern (Figure 15.2).

Figure 15.1

Figure 15.2

Prepare the patterns

At this point, you will have created a snug-fitting strapless design. This is now used to develop the patterns for the corselette and the bodice of the gown.

Prepare the corselette pattern

Trace the strapless pattern you've created, leaving a minimum 2.5cm (1") seam allowance at the opening and the upper edge. Mark the waistline, the bone placements and a stitching line 6mm (¼") above the lower edge. This is where the boning will end to allow for the lower edge finish.

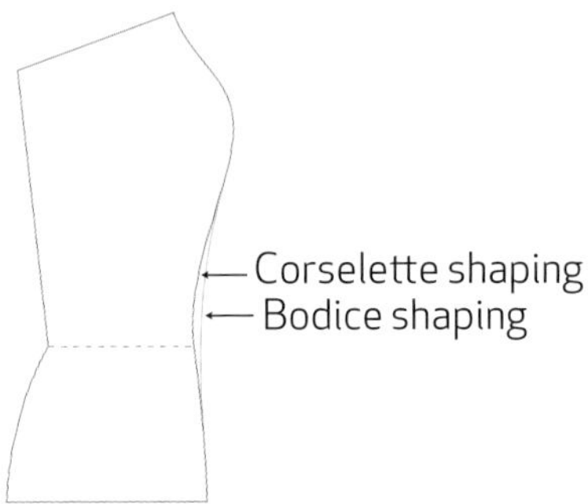

Figure 15.3

Prepare the bodice and skirt patterns

Make a second tracing of the pattern from the upper edge to the waistline, excluding the bust dart, then create a full pattern piece for the centre front panel. As a personal preference, the shaping under the bust can be softened (Figure 15.3). Mark the upper seam as a roll line and add a 2.5cm (1") extended facing.

The skirt, underskirt and lining use the same circular design and are taken from a Simplicity pattern. After the bodice is fitted, measure the waistline and choose a skirt size to match.

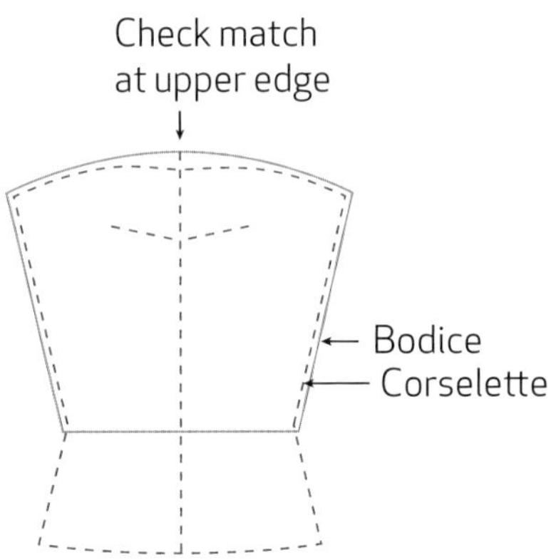

Figure 15.4

Sew and fit the toiles

Once the final patterns are drafted, it's worth checking their fit once more, particularly focusing on their fit together. Prepare and fit the toiles for the corselette and the bodice, pinning them together at the waist for the final fitting. Next, smooth the bodice over the corselette, pinning the upper edges together. If the corselette has a centre front dart, the length of the bodice may need to be adjusted at the centre front to match the length and the upper edge shaping of the corselette (Figure 15.4). Make any necessary adjustments here and to the overall fit of the bodice toile so that it sits smoothly over the corselette. In this design, it isn't necessary to make a toile for the skirt as it has ample ease, but check that the skirt waistline matches the bodice and the corselette. If a skirt with a slimmer silhouette is used, or the figure is curvaceous or asymmetrical, a skirt toile would be recommended.

Construct the inner corselette

Figure 15.5

The lined corselette is made with two layers of a tightly woven cotton cut on opposite grains and has thirteen spiral steel bones providing support and structure. The bones are housed in a combination of handmade tubular and cotton tape casings. When choosing the casings, consideration was given to making the bones less visible from the outside, through the light-coloured, smooth fashion fabric. Bones on the seamlines are cushioned by the seam allowances, while the bones placed mid panel are backed only with the outer layer of the corselette. Tubular casings add two extra layers under the bone, providing a buffer, so were a better choice for the mid-panel placements. Small bust pads made from cotton wadding and covered with silk crêpe de Chine are sewn to the inside and, as usual, there is a waist stay in Petersham ribbon. In this instance, the corselette doesn't have a separate fastening but instead shares a zipper with the gown bodice (Figure 15.5).

Sew the corselette shell

Prepare the two shells for a lined corselette and sufficient handmade tubular bone casings (Figure 15.6). (See 'Casings', page 64.) For ease, sew the mid-panel casings to the corselette before joining the panels, while they are still flat (Figure 15.7). Trim the seam allowances to about 1cm (⅜"), clip as necessary and then press them open. Thread trace the waistline as well as the upper and centre back, stitching lines on both shells, and attach hanging loops on the lining.

Figure 15.6

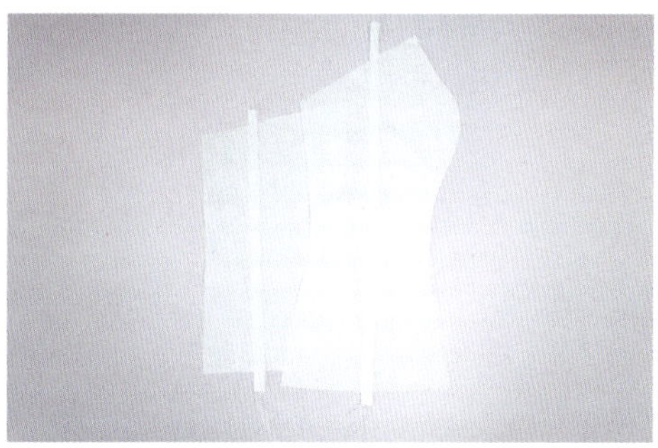

Figure 15.7

Figure 15.8

Add the bone casings

Centre cotton tape over the seams, running it from edge to edge, and stitch in place (Figure 15.8). Cut boning to fit each placement line, finishing the ends with a metal end cap.

Figure 15.9

Join the layers and finish the edges

1. Place the corselette and the lining with wrong sides together. Sew across the stitching line 6mm above the lower edge then bind the edge with seam binding (Figure 15.9).

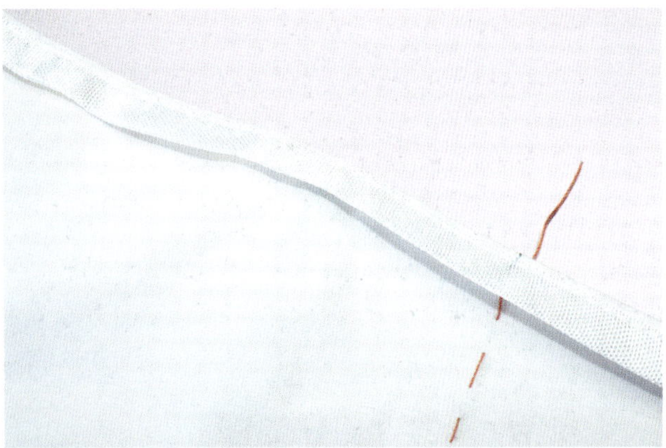

Figure 15.10

2. Insert the boning into the casings then baste across the upper edge of each casing to hold the boning.
3. Fold the lining up and match it with the corselette at the upper edge. Staystitch the upper stitching line through both layers. Trim the seam allowance and bind it with seam binding to stabilize and finish the edge in one step (Figure 15.10). Press the seam allowance to the inside then baste the two layers together at the centre back.

Sew the gown

Silk satin is the main fabric for the gown. The soft drape is perfect for the circular skirt but, to give the bodice enough structure, the satin will need to be underlined. The skirt has three layers: the outer skirt, a satin underskirt and a lining of crêpe de Chine. As the fabric is fairly transparent, care needs to be taken to achieve the same colour in the bodice as is created by the skirt layers. Testing several options for an underlining is important to ensure that the combination of fashion fabric and underlining gives the desired effect. In this project, the satin for the bodice was first backed with lightweight fusible interfacing to give it some stability. Next it was underlined with a layer of smooth dupion, which had lightweight fusible interfacing applied only within the seamlines. This provided further buffering for the seam allowances and boning. A regular invisible zipper fastens the skirt while a heavy-duty invisible zipper closes the bodice with the corselette.

Assemble the bodice

Interface and underline the bodice, thread tracing the stitching lines. Join the panels, trim the seam allowances and press them open, clipping as necessary.

Prepare the skirt

Cut the three skirt layers (main, underskirt and lining) and staystitch the waistlines. As the skirt sides are considerably off grain, it's necessary to hang the pieces for twenty-four hours before sewing. Sew each skirt layer, leaving an opening at the centre back (use French seams for a clean finish). Next, place the underskirt inside the main skirt, basting them together along the waistline and the back opening. Install an invisible zipper through both layers, setting it 1cm (⅜") below the waistline (Figure 15.11). Lastly, slip the lining inside the underskirt, wrong sides together, and baste to the skirt waistline. Turn in the opening seam allowances and slipstitch to the zipper.

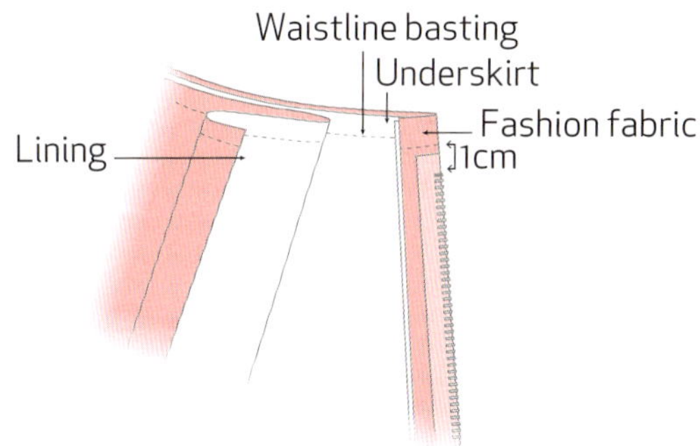

Figure 15.11

Join the skirts and bodice

First baste and then sew the skirt and the bodice together. It is essential to carefully align the skirt zipper with the centre back seam position on the bodice (Figure 15.12). Press the seam towards the bodice.

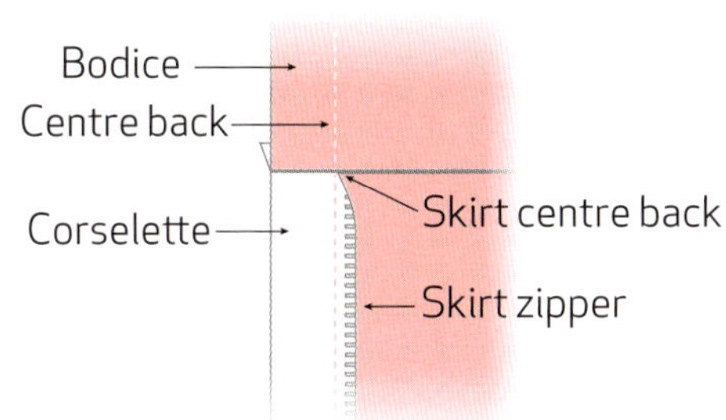

Figure 15.12

Join the inner corselette and gown

With the two garments almost finished, they are ready to be joined and have the fastening installed.

Join the bodice to the corselette

1. Slip the corselette inside the gown. Turn the bodice down and match the waistline seam to the placement line on the corselette (Figure 15.13).
2. Hand sew along the seamline through all layers (Figure 15.14).

Figure 15.13

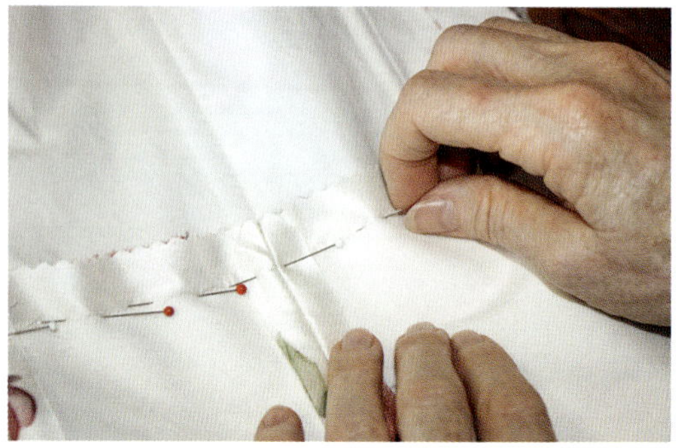

Figure 15.14

3. Turn the bodice up, matching the upper edge of the corselette to the roll line on the gown. Slipstitch the corselette in place along the roll line, taking care to catch the underlining only (Figure 15.15).

Figure 15.15

4. Match the corselette and the gown along the centre back seam and baste through all layers. Trim the bodice facing to about 2cm (¾") and turn to the inside over the upper edge of the corselette (Figure 15.16).

Figure 15.16

5. Stitch it to the corselette lining and then cover the raw edge with ribbon, handstitching it in place (Figure 15.17).

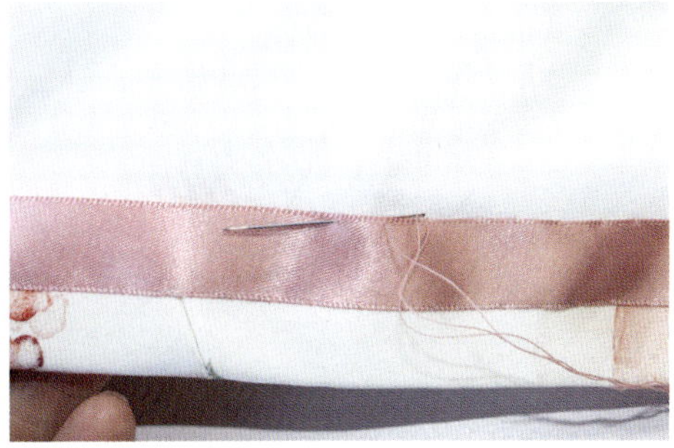

Figure 15.17

Install the zipper

Figure 15.18

Set the zipper 1cm (⅜") below the upper edge, and baste in place through all layers to the waistline, continuing below the waist in the corselette only, keeping the skirt free (Figure 15.18). Stitch in place, allowing the excess zipper length to hang below the corselette. For a neat finish, slip-stitch the zipper tape to the seam allowance.

Apply the finishing details

1. Bind the centre back seam allowances and the zipper end with seam binding. Sew a hook and eye above the zipper and then stitch the upper seam allowances to the corselette for about 2.5cm (1") (Figure 15.19).
2. Prepare and attach the waist stay, placing the lower edge on the waistline and securing it to the bone casings (Figure 15.20).

Figure 15.19

Figure 15.20

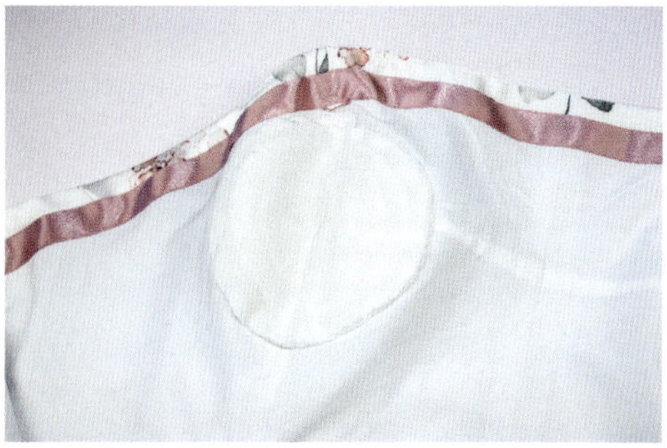

Figure 15.21

3. Place the bust enhancers in position, smoothing the corselette over the padding. Pin in place then slipstitch them to the lining (Figure 15.21).

Hem the skirts

Try on the gown, mark the length and sew a narrow hem on all skirt layers.

Bust enhancers

Bust enhancers can be purchased or custom-made to your preferred size, shape and thickness. To make your own, use the corselette pattern pieces for the side front and centre front. Cotton, bamboo or wool wadding (batting) are suitable choices for the padding.

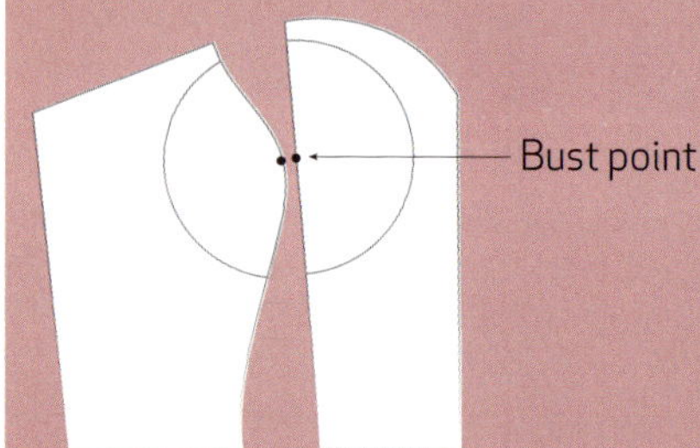

Step 1

From the bust point on each piece, draw a circle 7.5cm (3") in diameter (the approximate bust circumference for a B cup).

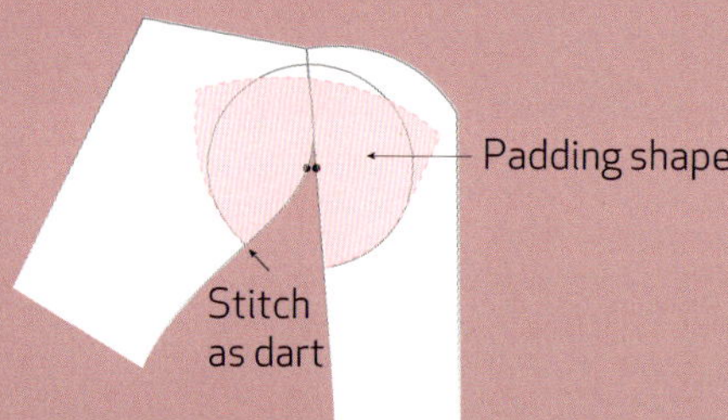

Step 2

Overlap the side front and the centre front on the seamline from the upper edge as far as possible and secure. Using the bust circle as a guide, draw the desired padding shape, making sure that it is set back from the upper edge.

Step 3

Trace the pattern piece and cut the layers from padding. Repeat the process, gradually reducing the size of each consecutive shape until the desired thickness is reached.

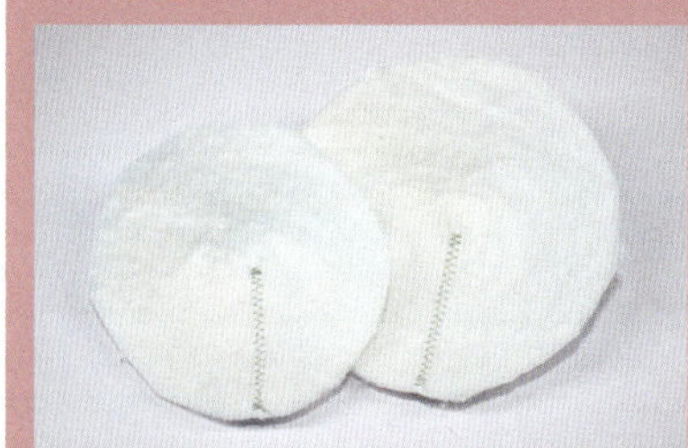

Step 4

Align the sides of the dart and zigzag them together.

Step 5

Layer the smallest two pieces and join with loose stitches then add the larger layers in turn.

Step 6

Cover with lightweight cotton or silk cut from the largest pattern size.

16

The Lilac Cocktail Gown

With soft hues and metallic highlights, this slim-fitting cocktail gown features a mid-thigh slit and a bodice cut revealing the corselette underneath. The corselette supports the bodice from the waist and midriff seams and the side closure gives a clean finish at the back.

This design demonstrates several different techniques and is one of the more challenging projects presented in this book. The difficulty comes from the method of developing the corselette pattern and the precision required when joining the gown and the corselette. We'll take a look at how to develop a pattern for both the gown and the hip-length corselette from a pattern for a panelled sheath dress with a waist seam. This involves a few more steps and most likely more than one toile will be needed to achieve a good fit. The double-layer corselette has plastic boning installed in casings and we'll explore creating and applying the corselette overlay. As this design prevents the two being joined at the upper edge, we will be joining them by hand through the torso, leaving the upper edges unattached.

Prepare the patterns

The pattern work for this design involves adapting the original pattern to create both the corselette and the gown patterns. A McCall's pattern for a strapless evening gown is the starting point for this project. The 'Create It' design has princess-seamed bodice and skirt options joining with a seam at the waist. A waist-length corselette could be created from the bodice pattern alone, but instead we will create a hip-length design to smooth and shape the lower torso under the slim-fitting skirt.

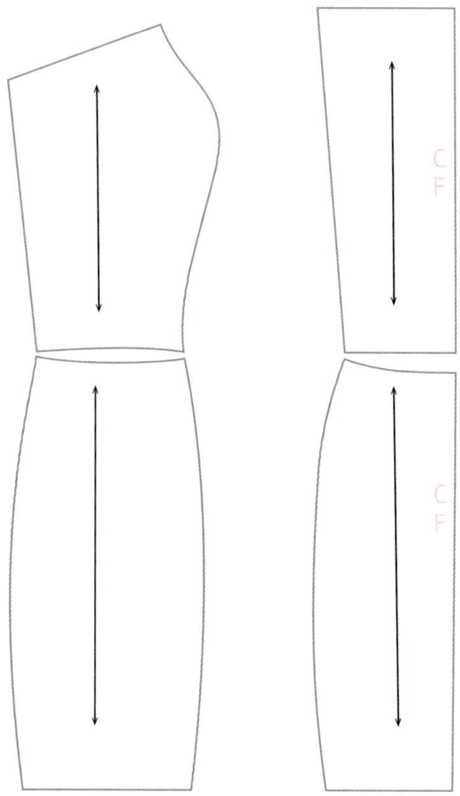

Figure 16.1

Create the hip-length corselette pattern

Copy the bodice panels, extending them to the high hip using the skirt panels as a guide (Figure 16.1). The fit and seam placement, particularly in the lower torso, will be refined during the toile fitting. Add a seam and a 1.6cm (⅝") dart at the centre front, then lower the upper edge 1cm (⅜"). Place the centre back on the fold and move the closure to the side.

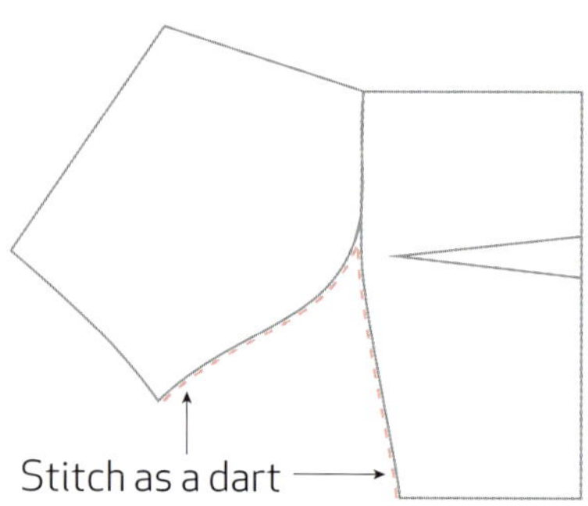

Figure 16.2

Create the corselette overlay

After the corselette fit is established with the toile, trace the corrected pattern from the upper edge to the midriff line. For a smoother finish at the upper edge, remove the princess seams by joining the front and side front panels at the upper edge and sewing the lower part of the seam as a dart. Smooth the upper edge and add a 2.5cm (1") extended facing then add a seam allowance at the lower edge (Figure 16.2). Join the two back panels in the same way to create a single piece. Smooth the upper edge then add the extended facing and a seam allowance at the lower edge.

Modify the pattern for the gown design

To create the new design, some simple changes to the original pattern are made.

Divide the bodice

Trace the bodice panels, placing the centre back on the fold and moving the closure to the left side. Mark a seamline on each bodice panel about 7cm (2¾") above the waist seam (just below the underbust). Divide each panel into an upper section and a lower section, adding seam allowances to the new seamlines on each upper bodice panel (Figure 16.3).

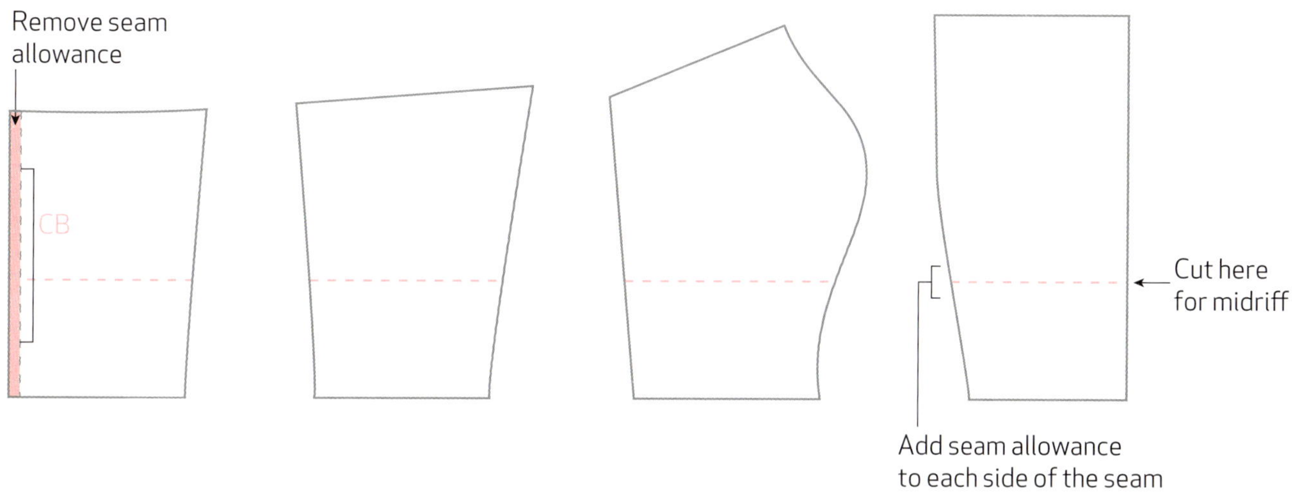

Figure 16.3

Create the midriff

Join the princess seams on the lower bodice panels to create a front and a back midriff. Smooth the joins then add seam allowances to the newly created seamlines (Figure 16.4).

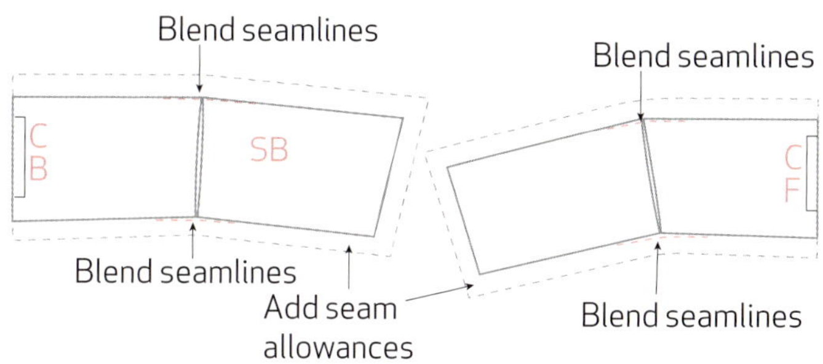

Figure 16.4

Figure 16.5

Prepare the upper bodice

Add a seam at the centre front and copy the dart from the corselette, folding it out to retain the same length at the centre front. Draft the front opening, in this case a V shape which is raised above the original upper edge at the points (Figure 16.5). To create a seamless piece for the upper back, align the princess seams at the lower edge, leaving a little ease at the upper edge. Finally, transfer the placement line for the midriff to the corselette pattern.

Modify the skirt

Mark a slit on the skirt left front princess seam and move the zipper to the side.

Sew and fit the toiles

Creating toiles for both the corselette and the gown is essential, especially in this more complex design. To achieve a good fit and elegant style lines, a second toile of one or both garments may be necessary.

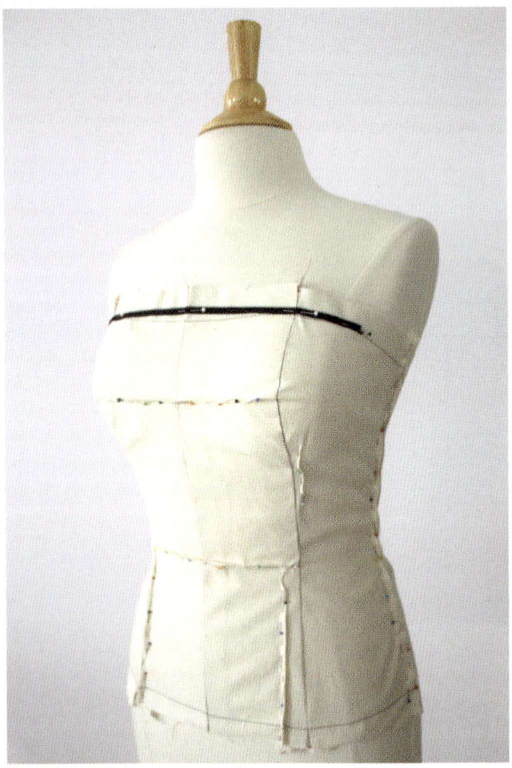

Figure 16.6

Refine the corselette fit

Ensure that the corselette is a snug fit, taking special note below the waist where it needs less ease than the skirt pattern it was developed from. Adjust the seams, forming a pleasing line. Mark the upper and the lower edge, check the depth and placement of the front darts and assess the boning needs. In this case, extra boning is added in the side front and side back panels to provide sufficient support (Figure 16.6).

Fit the gown toile

Transfer any changes made to the corselette above the waistline to the toile for the gown as the two garments must match through this area. Fit the gown toile alone as well as over the corselette to check the overall fit. The bodice should fit closely over the corselette through the midriff, while the upper bodice has a little ease over the fit of the corselette. Make sure that the waist and midriff seams on the gown match the placement lines on the corselette. Review the design of the bodice and the corselette at the centre front, refining it as necessary.

Construct the inner corselette

The corselette is constructed from a double layer of silk taffeta cut on opposite grains and has eleven reinforced (German) plastic bones housed in satin bias tape casings. It's covered with a satin overlay and fastens at the side with fourteen hand-sewn hooks and eyes (Figure 16.7). Seam binding and Petersham ribbon both play a role to cover and stabilize areas, while lace trims the lower edge.

Figure 16.7

Sew the corselette shell

Using the process for a double-layer woven corselette, create the shell, placing the opening on the left side. Thread trace the midriff, waistline and left side seams as well as the mid-panel bone placements (Figure 16.8). Trim and clip the seam allowances, press them open and finish the raw edges.

Figure 16.8

Add the bone casings

To form the casings, centre bias tape over each seam and bone placement line running from edge to edge and stitch in place (Figure 16.9). To avoid the centre front bone being noticeable at the upper edge, it will finish at bust level. Stitch across the casing at bust level to mark where the boning needs to end (Figure 16.10).

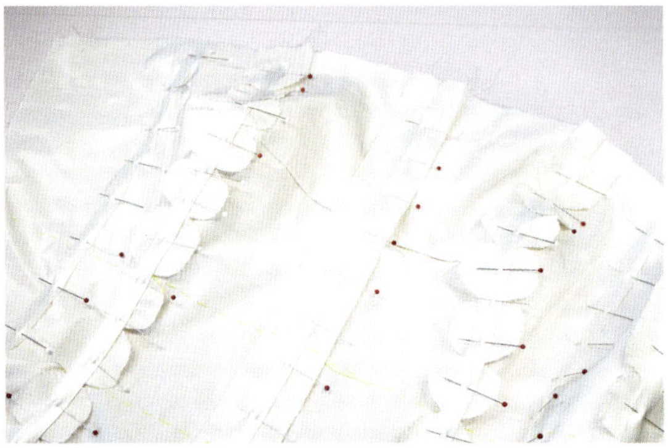

Figure 16.9

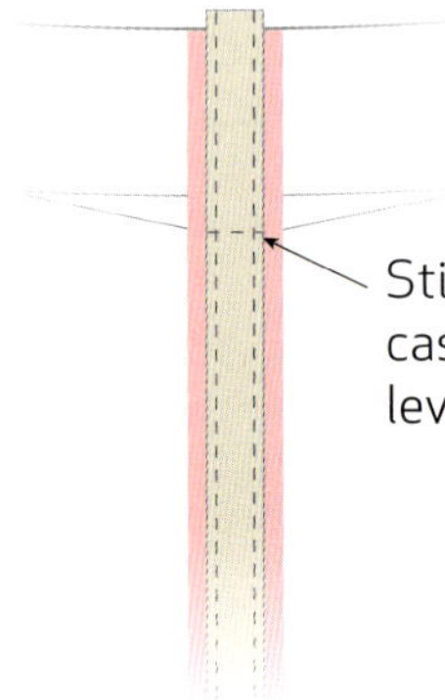

Figure 16.10

Install the boning and finish the edges

Stabilize the upper edge by centring seam binding over the stitching line and machine stitch it in place, trimming the seam allowance to 1.3cm (½") (Figure 16.11). Cut boning to fit each casing, finish the ends and insert the boning in the casings. Machine stitch the lower edge to secure the boning then trim and finish the raw edge. On the inside, hand sew hemming lace along the lower edge (Figure 16.12).

Figure 16.11

Figure 16.12

Sew and apply the overlay

Prepare the overlay by stitching the darts and the right side seam. Place the wrong side of the overlay on the right side of the corselette, matching placement and seamlines (Figure 16.13).

Stitch it to the corselette at the midriff seam using a running stitch, before basting the outer edges together by hand. Cover the lower raw edges with seam binding for 5cm (2") either side of the opening, to neaten them (see Figure 16.16).

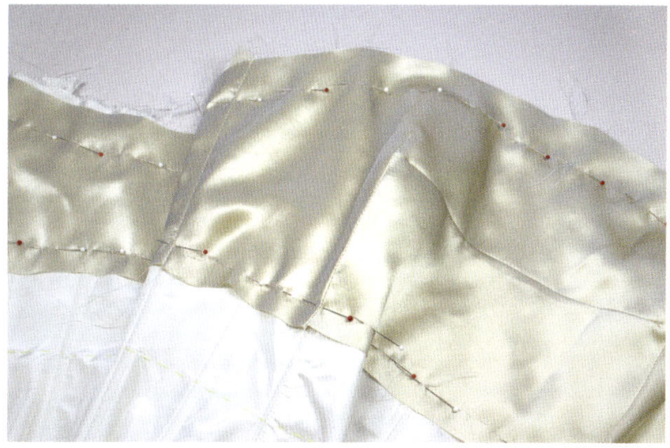

Figure 16.13

Add the fastening

1. To reinforce the side opening, cut 1.5cm-wide (⅝"-wide) Petersham ribbon the length of each side of the opening and shape it with steam to match the curve of the seamline. Baste it next to the seamline (Figure 16.14) and then turn the seam allowance to the inside over the tape and stitch through all layers 1cm (⅜") from the folded edge.

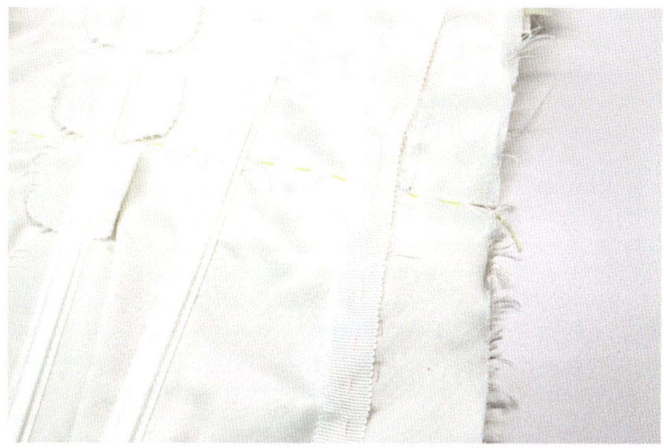

Figure 16.14

2. Stitch hooks to the front edge and eyes to the back edge, placing the top pair 3mm (⅛") below the upper edge, taking care to stitch into the ribbon but not through to the outside (Figure 16.15).

Figure 16.15

Figure 16.16

3. Cover the hooks with seam binding, hand sewing it in place. Prepare a length of 2.5cm-wide (1"-wide) Petersham ribbon to fit the back edge, shape with steam as before and finish the ends with seam binding. Slipstitch it in place behind the eyes to cover them and form an extension (Figure 16.16).

Figure 16.17

Finish the upper edge

Attach hanging loops at the upper edge. Fold the extended facing to the inside along the roll line (staystitch just inside the fold and clip if necessary), turn under the raw edge then slipstitch the edge to the corselette inner layer (Figure 16.17).

Sew the gown

A lightweight jacquard is used to construct the gown. It is underlined in cotton voile to provide some added support for the slim-fitting, structured design. The skirt and the upper bodice are lined with silk satin and a regular zipper is hand sewn into the side in a lapped application. Baste the underlined gown together for a final fitting with the corselette, making any necessary changes before proceeding.

Sew the upper bodice

Sew the panels together for the upper bodice and the lining, then join the two together at the upper edge and the front opening. To support the front opening, bend a length of zigzag wire to match the centre front angle and hand stitch to the underlining (Figure 16.18). Fold the lining to the inside and understitch it by hand (Figure 16.19).

Figure 16.18

Figure 16.19

Sew the midriff and skirt

Join the midriff sections and assemble the skirt, leaving openings on the left side for the zipper and the front slit. Due to the springy nature of this fabric, catchstitching the seams to the underlining encourages them to stay flat. Finally, join the three sections by sewing the waist and midriff seams, keeping the bodice lining free.

Install the zipper

Baste the zipper in place by hand in a lapped application and perform a final fitting before sewing the zipper permanently.

Complete the lining

Sew the skirt lining then slip it into the skirt, wrong sides together. Hand stitch the lining to the skirt just next to the waistline seam and slipstitch it to the zipper tape. Turn down the bodice lining and fold in the side seam allowances. Slipstitch the lining to the zipper tape and baste the lower edge to the midriff seamline. To neaten the end of the midriff, which will be visible, apply a 5cm (2") piece of lining to both ends (Figure 16.20).

Figure 16.20

Figure 16.21

Finish the zipper

To secure the lapped edge over the zipper, sew a hook and thread bar onto the gown at the upper edge and the waistline (Figure 16.21).

Figure 16.22

Complete the hem and slit facing

Turn up and secure the hem to the underlining. Slip-stitch the lining in place at the lower edge and the front slit. On the inside, sew a metal bar (from a hook set) at the top of the slit to help prevent it tearing (Figure 16.22).

Join the inner corselette and gown

You will now have both the corselette and the gown almost complete, ready to hand sew together.

Attach the corselette to the gown

Slip the gown over the corselette, matching the waist seam to the placement line on the corselette. Turn down the bodice and stitch the seam allowance to the corselette, stopping 2.5cm (1") from the side opening (Figure 16.23). Turn the bodice up and smooth the gown over the corselette, matching the midriff seam with the placement line on the corselette. From the outside, stitch invisibly through all layers, stopping 2.5cm (1") from the side opening.

Figure 16.23

Attach the waist stay

Prepare the waist stay. Secure it to each bone casing, with the lower edge of the stay resting on the waistline (Figure 16.24).

Figure 16.24

Apply the finishing touches

Smooth the bodice over the corselette, matching its placement line with the upper edge of the corselette. Fasten the bodice to the corselette on the side front seams with French tacks set 1cm (⅜") below the corselette upper edge (Figure 16.25).

Figure 16.25

Glossary

Armscye The armhole.

Baste Sewing the garment together by hand or machine with temporary stitches so that the garment can be fitted and adjusted before stitching it permanently.

Bias grain The grainline at a 45° angle to the lengthwise grain.

Bodice 1. An article of woman's clothing which extends from the shoulder to the waist. 2. The part of a dress above the waist, not including the sleeves or collar. 3. Historically, it has also been used to describe a vest-like garment that was laced at the front.

Catchstitch A hand-sewn stitch made in the shape of an 'X' used to keep one edge flat against an underneath layer. Commonly used to secure a seam or hem allowance.

CB Centre back.

Centred zipper A zipper sewn into a seam where the seam edges meet evenly in the centre of the zipper.

CF Centre front.

Closure The opening in a garment or the mechanism used to close the garment, such as a zipper, buttons or hooks and eyes.

Corselette A type of woman's undergarment combining a lightly boned, low hip-length corset and a brassiere. In this book, a corselette generally refers to a princess-seamed, boned foundation garment attached inside a garment and is used interchangeably with inner corselette.

Corset A tightly fitting, boned undergarment worn to reduce the waist and mould the body semi-permanently into a desired shape, either for fashion or for medical purposes.

Crosswise grain The threads which are at a 90° angle to the selvage.

Edgestitch A row of stitches sewn 3mm (⅛") from the edge to secure the layers.

Facing A piece of fabric used to cover and finish the raw edge of a garment, such as the neckline, armscye or opening. The facing may be a separate shaped piece of fabric sewn on, an extension of the pattern piece itself, or a tape or ribbon.

Fastening The mechanism used to close a garment, for example a zipper, buttons or hooks and eyes.

Foundation garment A generic term used to describe a woman's undergarment worn to give support or shape to the body, such as a girdle, a brassiere or a corset. Its purpose is to support the body in a more fashionable manner.

French tack A length of chain stitches used to loosely connect two points. Also called a thread chain.

Girdle 1. Historically, a close-fitting belt which girded (encircled) the lower torso and was worn over loose-fitting outer garments. 2. Contemporary use: an undergarment worn to slim and shape the lower torso. Similar in function to a corset but less restrictive.

Hand overcasting A small, evenly spaced diagonal stitch sewn along the edge of the fabric to prevent fraying.

Hemline The lower edge of the garment. It may be a fold or a seamline.

Horsehair A type of netting used to stiffen and give body to areas of the garment such as the hemline.

Interfacing A fabric used to stiffen and stabilize the edges of a garment.

Lengthwise grain The threads in the fabric which run parallel to the selvage.

Lower edge The finished edge of the corselette.

Notions Notions are the extra supplies needed to complete a sewing project. The notions discussed here are the zippers, tapes, and hooks and eyes.

Placket A finished opening in the garment to allow for ease of dressing.

Pre-shrink To wash and dry, steam press or dry clean a fabric element of the garment prior to its use, such as the fabric, tapes and ribbons.

Pressing To use heat and possibly steam to smooth and flatten the fabric or part of the garment by lifting and placing the iron on the fabric in an up-and-down (not side-to-side) motion.

Prick stitch A type of backstitch in which only a small amount of thread shows on the right side of the garment. It is used to set a zipper or understitch a facing or lining by hand.

SB Side back.

Self-fabric The same fabric as the garment.

Selvage The narrow, tightly woven border that runs down each lengthwise edge of the fabric and stops it from fraying.

SF Side front.

Shape To use heat and steam to mould the fabric into a form by stretching or shrinking it or pressing it over a curved surface.

Slipstitch A hand stitch used to hold two layers flat against one another.

Stay A tape or ribbon sewn to a seamline or edge to stabilize it.

Stays 1. A boned undergarment worn during the seventeenth and eighteenth centuries to shape and support the body. From the nineteenth century they began to be referred to as a corset. 2. The whalebones used to stiffen a stay or a corset.

Staystitch A line of stitching sewn in the seam allowance just next to the seamline to prevent the fabric from stretching during the construction of the garment.

Thread bar Strands of thread anchored to the fabric at each end then covered with a blanket or buttonhole stitch. Used as loops for fastening buttons and metal hooks, as well as for holding elastic stays, hanging loops or belts in place. Also known as a thread loop.

Thread tracing A basting stitch used to mark the stitching lines on a garment.

Toile A mock-up of the garment made in an inexpensive fabric to trial the design and fit. Also known as a muslin.

Understitching A row of hand or machine stitches sewn close to the edge of a facing or lining (keeping the garment free) to secure the seam allowances underneath and prevent them from rolling towards the outside.

Upper edge The finished edge of the corselette or garment. It can be a seam or foldline.

Wadding A layer of insulation used between fabric layers. It can be made from cotton, wool, bamboo or polyester and is commonly used in quilting projects. Also known as batting.

Polyester
1000 m

Resources

Many of the sewing supplies needed for these projects will be readily available at your favourite local or online fabric and haberdashery store. Following is a small list of companies, curated by regions, where you can access the patterns and specialized products to build your inner corselette.

Australia and New Zealand
NZ Corsetry Supplies,
www.nzcorsetry.co.nz

Sewing patterns by Vogue, McCall's and Simplicity,
www.sewdirect.com.au

North America
Farthingales Corset Making Supplies,
www.farthingalescorsetmakingsupplies.com

Richard the Thread,
www.richardthethread.com

Sewing patterns by Vogue, McCall's and Simplicity,
www.simplicity.com

United Kingdom
Vena Cava Design,
www.venacavadesign.co.uk

Sewing patterns by Vogue, McCall's and Simplicity,
www.sewdirect.com

Bibliography and Further Reading

Sewing techniques

Harris, Kristina, ed. *Authentic Victorian Dressmaking Techniques*. New York: Dover Publications, 1999.

Khalje, Susan. *Bridal Couture*. Iola, WI: Krause Publications, 1997.

Shaeffer, Claire B. *Couture Sewing Techniques*. Newtown, CT: Taunton Press, 2011.

Corsetry techniques

Bremble, Julia. *Corset Making: For Beginners to Intermediate*. Honiton: Rainbow Disks, 2012.

Sparks, Linda. *The Basics of Corset Building: A Handbook for Beginners*. New York: St Martin's Griffin, 2005.

Fabrics

Betzina, Sandrax. *More Fabric Savvy*. Newtown, CT: Taunton Press, 2004.

Khalje, Susan. *Linen and Cotton*. Newton, CT: Taunton Press, 1999.

Vogue and Butterick Patterns, eds. *A to Z of Fabrics*. New York: Butterick Company, 1994.

Historical fashion

Edwards, Lydia. *How to Read a Dress: A Guide to Changing Fashion from the 16th to the 20th Century*. London: Bloomsbury Academic, 2017.

Hill, Colleen. *Exposed: A History of Lingerie*. New Haven, CT: Yale University Press, 2014.

Palmer, Alexandra. *Christian Dior: History and Modernity 1947–1959*. Toronto: Royal Ontario Museum, 2018.

Fitting

Liechty, E., J. Rasband and D. Pottberg-Steineckert. *Fitting and Pattern Alteration: A Multi-method Approach to the Art of Style Selection, Fitting, and Alteration*, 2nd edn. New York: Fairchild Books, 2010. (A 4th edition of this book is available.)

Threads magazine. *Fitting for Every Figure*. Newtown, CT: Taunton Press, 2012.

Veblen, Sarah. *The Complete Photo Guide to Perfect Fitting*. Minneapolis, MN: Creative Publishing International, 2012.

Drafting

Amaden-Crawford, Amanda. *Pattern Making Made Easy*, 2nd edn. Hansville, WA: Amaden-Crawford, 2007.

Haggar, Ann. *Pattern Cutting for Lingerie, Beachwear and Leisurewear*, 2nd edn. Oxford: Blackwell Publishing, 2004.

Powell, Pamela. *Lingerie Design: A Complete Course*. London: Laurence King Publishing, 2016.

Websites

In-House Patterns
www.inhousepatternsstudio.com
A great online resource for fitting and pattern-making tutorials, including excellent tutorials on fitting the bust.

Museum at FIT
www.fitnyc.edu
A specialized fashion museum in New York City offering exhibitions, publications and educational programmes. It also has an extensive online collection to view.

The Underpinnings Museum
www.underpinningsmuseum.com
An online museum documenting the history of lingerie through detailed photography and accompanying technical information.

Witness2Fashion
www.witness2fashion.wordpress.com
A blog focusing on the history and significance of everyday clothing, including documentation of the evolution of women's undergarments.

Index

Page numbers in italics refer to figures and tables

U

W

Z